Christina Rossetti and the Poetry of Discovery

Christina Rossetti

AND THE POETRY OF DISCOVERY

Katherine J. Mayberry

Louisiana State University Press
Baton Rouge and London

Copyright © 1989 by Louisiana State University Press
All rights reserved
Manufactured in the United States of America
First printing

98 97 96 95 94 93 92 91 90 89   5 4 3 2 1

Designer: Laura Roubique Gleason
Typeface: Granjon
Typesetter: The Composing Room of Michigan, Inc.
Printer & Binder: Thomson-Shore, Inc.

Library of Congress Cataloging-in-Publication Data

Mayberry, Katherine J., 1950–
    Christina Rossetti and the poetry of discovery / Katherine J.
Mayberry.
        p. cm.
    Bibliography: p.
    Includes index.
    ISBN 0-8071-1529-0 (alk. paper)
    1. Rossetti, Christina Georgina, 1830–1894—Criticism and
interpretation.   I. Title.
PR5238.M38   1989
821'.8—dc20   89-33163
                                                       CIP

The paper in this book meets the guidelines for permanence and durability of the
Committee on Production Guidelines for Book Longevity of the Council on
Library Resources. ∞

To the memory of
Rowland L. Collins

Contents

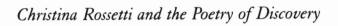

Christina Rossetti and the Poetry of Discovery

Introduction

The tension and incongruity in Christina Rossetti's life and work are apparent after only a glance. Most striking is the contrast between the luxuriance of the poetry and the asceticism of the life. The incongruity is not uncommon, particularly among women writers, but it is no less intriguing for its prevalence. It is probably this very contradiction that has elicited the many hypotheses about the personal origins of the provocative works of Dickinson, Rossetti, the Brontë sisters, and others. Surely few can read Dickinson's "I got so I could hear his name" (No. 293) or "I cannot live with You" (No. 640), or Rossetti's "Convent Threshold" or "A Birthday" without some curiosity about the personal referents of the poems. This is poetry that invites, even demands, speculation about the circumstances that inspired it.

In the case of Christina Rossetti, far more attention has been paid to the biographical circumstances than to the poetry itself. Of the fourteen full-length studies published on Rossetti since her death in 1894, twelve are biographies, many intent upon identifying the "mystery man" of the love poems. Between 1930 and 1980, criticism reflected the bias toward biography. Rossetti scholarship during this comparatively dry period attempted, not to explicate the love poetry, but to translate it into biography.[1] During these same years, little attention was paid to Rossetti's devotional verse, which constitutes almost half of her canon.

1. See especially Lona Mosk Packer, *Christina Rossetti* (Berkeley, 1963); and Germaine Greer, Introduction to *Goblin Market*, by Christina Rossetti (New York, 1975), vii–xxxvi.

Given the biographical preoccupation that Rossetti's poetry seems to elicit from its readers, it is not surprising that the New Critical approach was never applied to her work. Implicit in this oversight is the assumption that Rossetti's poetry is only accessible when examined in terms of historical or biographical contexts. For the strict textual critic, such context-dependent poetry was insignificant. It is true that many of Rossetti's devotional poems are illuminated by our familiarity with a particular phase in English religious history,[2] and that many of her secular poems are enriched by an understanding of Victorian sexual politics, but Rossetti's poetry is far from entirely context dependent. Christina Rossetti was a gifted artist whose skills as a poet have, until very recently, been consistently overlooked, even by the most well intentioned critics seeking to revive her flagging reputation. Many of her best poems (including some that could be called great) respond well to the *analyse du texte* method. At its best, her poetry speaks clearly and requires no reference to its contexts.

But the textual method will, finally, be limiting if our aim is wider than a judgment of the technical merit of the poetry. This method can teach us little about the poet herself, about her relationship to her work, about the transmutation of the raw data of her life into art. And at this comparatively early stage in Christina Rossetti scholarship, these issues require attention. Rossetti's poetry is important for its artistic merit, but it is also valuable for its documentation (however refracted and revised) of the conditions that so profoundly influenced the artistic and personal development of the rare phenomenon that Christina Rossetti represents: a willingly unmarried, professional, successful woman poet in Victorian England.

Rossetti's poetry is most resonant when examined in terms of its workmanship *and* its biographical and historical contexts. If we are to understand and appreciate the poetry fully, we must understand the circumstances surrounding and informing its composition, particularly the anomaly of Rossetti's choice of career and her attitude toward that choice. In a case such as Rossetti's, where the very acts of writing and publishing poetry were extraordinary, the life must be seen as a foil to the art. The fault in the earlier biographical readings of Rossetti's poetry is not so much in the biographical impulse as in the methodology and objective.

2. Jerome J. McGann, "The Religious Poetry of Christina Rossetti," *Critical Inquiry,* X (1983), 127–44.

The tendency has been to scan the biography for clues to the identity of the people and events suggested in the poems, to offer inconsequential explanations of the poetry developed from simplistic correlations of biographical conjecture with a handful of particularly provocative poems. Even if we could establish identities through such a biographical search (and William Michael Rossetti was too protective a trustee of his sister's reputation to allow us to do this with any certainty), such an exercise would not help us penetrate beyond the surface of the poems.

Happily, scholars are coming to recognize that Rossetti's work contains issues more crucial than the biographical referents of its people and situations. Two pressing questions are why Christina Rossetti was a poet, and how she used her art to reconcile her choice of career with the social norms of her day. For the most part, the answers to these questions are to be found in the poems themselves, in their imagery, themes, dramatic representations, and insistent repetitions. This study addresses these issues and establishes Rossetti's skill as a poet through an examination of her poetry.

Because much of the following discussion relies on information about Rossetti's life, career, and critical reputation, the first chapter summarizes Rossetti's life and surveys the last fifty years of Rossetti scholarship. The remainder of the book investigates the relationship between Rossetti's poetic activity, her perception of her role as a woman in Victorian society, and her understanding of the functions of poetry. From this investigation, Christina Rossetti emerges as an artist at the same time unorthodox and conventional, iconoclastic and pious, but always committed to discovering an aesthetic that would resolve these tensions and justify her unconventional choice of vocation.

ONE

Biographical and Critical Background

 hristina Georgina Rossetti was born in London on December 5, 1830.[1] One of the most remarkable features of a childhood at the same time typical and unusual was her immediate family. Her father, Gabriele Giuseppe Rossetti, himself a poet, was a passionate and flamboyant man, zealously dedicated to the cause of Italian freedom and to his eccentric scholarship on Dante. According to his son William Michael Rossetti, he "was an earnest advocate of free nationalities, free institutions, independence of thought . . . [who] suffered in the cause of constitutional liberty."[2] In the Rossetti household, Gabriele's emotional intemperance was moderated by the sensible calmness of his wife, Frances Lavinia Polidori. Christina and her three siblings, Maria Francesca (1827–1876), Dante Gabriel (1828–1882), and William Michael (1829–1919), all of whom exhibited precocious literary ability, spent their early life in intimate and uninterrupted development of their talents. The four children, particularly the girls, lived in relative seclusion from the social, political, and cultural currents of Victorian London. While William and Dante Gabriel attended King's College School, Christina and Maria were educated at home by their mother. When Christina was about twenty years old, she took drawing lessons at Ford Madox Brown's North London School of Design, but this was the only formal training she ever received outside her home.

1. The primary sources of this biographical sketch are Packer, *Christina Rossetti,* and Georgina Battiscombe, *Christina Rossetti: A Divided Life* (London, 1981).
2. William Michael Rossetti, *Some Reminiscences of William Michael Rossetti* (New York, 1906), I, 125.

What society the Rossettis did entertain was not typically Victorian. As R. D. Waller recognized, the Rossettis were "very much a household apart." The Rossetti house on Charlotte Street was the meeting place for a group of passionately political Italian expatriates like Gabriele Rossetti himself. According to Waller, "The company in Charlotte Street was probably among the most interesting and bizarre in London." Among the regular Italian visitors were "the exiled General Michele Carrascosa . . . Count Carlo Pepoli, the soprano Giuditta Pasta, the antifeminist author Guido Sorelli, the cellist Dragonetti, the sculptor Sangiovanni, the lexicographer Petroni, the violinist Paganini."[3] During Christina's adolescence, her limited but extraordinary circle of acquaintances widened to include the now-famous group of talented young artists (the self-named Pre-Raphaelite Brotherhood) who frequented the Rossetti household in the late 1840s. Although Christina contributed poems to the P.R.B. journal, the *Germ,* there was always considerable distance between the sister and the "brothers." At whose insistence this distance was maintained is uncertain. Holman Hunt and John Millais, two of the founding members of the Brotherhood, objected to Dante Gabriel's suggestion that Christina be admitted as an honorary brother. Christina finally resolved the disagreement by refusing even to have her poems read aloud (in her absence) at the P.R.B. meetings.

The years between 1842 and 1849 were marked by enormous disruptions in Christina's life and by dramatic change in her outlook on the world. In 1843, Gabriele Rossetti became seriously ill and was forced to resign his teaching position at King's College, Lor don. This loss of income required other family members to find employment: Frances returned to teaching (her work before her marriage to Rossetti); Maria became a governess; and William Michael took a job at the Excise Office. Dante Gabriel's promising art career exempted him from a fate similar to his brother's, and Christina's youth and suddenly delicate health excused her from following Maria's lead. Although healthy as a child, Christina was also ill throughout this period and stayed at home, writing poetry and nursing her father. Gabriele Rossetti's health deteriorated for eleven years, and he was often close to death. In 1854, when Christina was twenty-three years old, Gabriele Rossetti died.

3. R. D. Waller, *The Rossetti Family, 1824–1854* (Manchester, England, 1932), 58, 75; Stanley Weintraub, *Four Rossettis: A Victorian Biography* (New York, 1977), 2.

Little has been written about Christina Rossetti's relationship with her father, but we can deduce that Gabriele Rossetti's illness played a crucial role in Christina's development. An attractive and passionate man, Gabriele Rossetti was one of only two men to play prominent roles in Christina's childhood (the other being her maternal grandfather, Gaetano Polidori, who died in 1853). During the years of Rossetti's illness, Christina was her father's primary caretaker and confidante. They experienced an intense, close relationship from which all other members of the family were of necessity excluded. William Bell Scott's famous description of his first meeting with Christina suggests the remarkable affinity that must have developed between father and daughter during this period:

I entered the small front parlour or dining room of the house, and found an old gentleman writing by the fire in a great chair, with a thick manuscript book open before him, and the largest snuff-box I ever saw beside it conveniently open. He had a black cap on his head furnished with a great peak or shade for the eyes, so that I saw his face only partially.

By the window was a high narrow reading-desk at which stood writing a slight girl with a serious regular profile, dark against the pallid wintry light without. This most interesting to me of the two inmates turned on my entrance, made the most formal and graceful curtsey, and resumed her writing, and the old gentleman signed to a chair for my sitting down. . . . Though I did not know that both of them—he and his daughter—were probably at that moment writing poetry of some sort and might wish me far enough, I left very soon.

This scene of father and daughter, completely alone in the warm and intimate front parlor, assiduously and companionably composing their poetry, reveals a bond between the two that must have affected Christina deeply. Exempted from earning a living, they were confederates in a craft that was tremendously important to them both. Under such circumstances, Christina's attachment to her father must have flourished. Certainly, she had no desire to relinquish her position as nurse, companion, and fellow artist; when her youth no longer excused her from joining the family's efforts to remain solvent, she became ill. At the age of fifteen, she developed vague physical complaints tentatively diagnosed as angina pectoris but never conclusively identified. These symptoms soon gave way to indications of consumption, which never actually developed, but were some time in abating.[4]

During this same period, Christina became absorbed in the highly formalized Tractarian Anglo-Catholicism, to which her mother and sister were also devoted. While we cannot be certain whether her growing preoccupation with religion was related to her father's condition, there is stark evidence that this period in Christina Rossetti's life *was* emotionally debilitating. Impetuous, temperamental, and charming as a child, Christina became retiring, self-critical, and morbid in her teenage years. Between the ages of sixteen and eighteen, Christina deteriorated mentally and physically. According to the physician attending her during this period, "She was then more or less out of her mind . . . (suffering in fact, from a form of insanity . . . a kind of religious mania)."[5] This is the only extant reference of its kind by a contemporary of Rossetti, but it appears to be documented by the poetry of the period, particularly by "Heart's Chill Between" (1848).

Complicating and no doubt contributing to the stress of this period in Christina's life was her engagement in 1848 to James Collinson, one of the least distinguished of the Pre-Raphaelite brothers. Collinson, a converted Roman Catholic when he met Christina, was only successful in his marriage suit after he left the Catholic church and joined Christina's Anglican Christ Church. The relationship between the two appears to have been no more remarkable than was Collinson himself. No correspondence between Christina and Collinson survives (none may have been written), but from other sources, including Christina's references to her fiancé in letters to family members, we can conclude that Christina was ambivalent about her impending marriage. When Collinson returned to Catholicism in late 1849—a faith that was anathema to the Anglo-Catholic Christina—she terminated the engagement.

Christina enjoyed her first public literary success during the period of her engagement to Collinson. In October of 1848, with the appearance of "Heart's Chill Between" in the *Anthenaeum,* her poetry was introduced to the greater literary public. From this time until her death in 1894, she saw

4. Packer, *Christina Rossetti,* 376–77; Waller, *The Rossetti Family,* 332.

5. James A. Kohl, "A Medical Comment on Christina Rossetti," *Notes and Queries,* CCXIII (1968), 423–24.

herself as a serious professional poet. After 1848, many more of the individual poems were printed in periodicals, but her first collection, *Goblin Market and Other Poems,* was not published until 1862. While Rossetti's poetry was successful throughout her career, this collection received the most critical acclaim. Her only volume actually to fail was *Commonplace,* a collection of short stories published in 1871. The later works, which were almost exclusively devoted to religious subjects, appealed to a more limited audience but nevertheless fared well on the public market. The last poetical volume to appear during Rossetti's lifetime, the 1893 *Verses,* went through three editions within a year of its first appearance.

From 1854 until 1866, Christina Rossetti led a comparatively quiet life, dividing her time between her three central interests: her art, her religion, and her family. These years were punctuated by only a few remarkable events. In 1854, Rossetti signed up to join the forces of Florence Nightingale at the Crimean front, but was rejected because of her youth. In 1860, she added to her professional, religious, and familial duties volunteer work at the Highgate House of Charity for "fallen women," which she continued until 1870. In 1861 and again in 1865, she traveled with her mother and William Michael to France and Italy, but for the most part she spent these years in London, living with her mother and sister.

In 1866, at the age of thirty-five, Christina received a second proposal of marriage, this time from Charles Bagot Cayley, a gentlemanly scholar and former student of her father's. It appears that Christina was a good deal more fond of Cayley than she had been of Collinson, but nevertheless she declined his proposal, once again on grounds of religious incompatibility. (Cayley was openly agnostic, Christina still a devout Anglo-Catholic.)

Literary tradition has assigned to Rossetti the role of sexual recluse; to many, her biography reveals a woman perhaps preternaturally reluctant to engage in a permanent sexual relationship. This impression may well be valid, though the etiology of Rossetti's reluctance requires careful investigation. It must be emphasized that despite Rossetti's lack of experience with men, she was a close and uncritical witness to a great number of relationships, many of them scandalous by Victorian standards, virtually all of them eventual failures. A participant herself in two failed relationships, she also watched the painful dissolution of the relationship between her brother Dante Gabriel and Lizzie Siddal. Christina could not have been unaware of Dante Gabriel's gradual disaffection from Lizzie or his later attachment to Janie Morris, herself unhappily married. In the 1850s, Christina watched her sister, Maria, suffer the pangs of an unrequited affection for John Ruskin. Even the comparatively staid William Michael was not exempt from the trials of disappointed love. In 1860, his long-standing hopes of marrying Henrietta Rintoul were dashed by her inexplicable severance of their engagement, an event that affected Christina deeply. More peripherally, Christina was aware of the sham marriage between William Bell Scott and Letitia Norquoy, and probably of John Ruskin and Effie Gray's divorce. And in her work with the "fallen women" of the Highgate House of Charity, she found sobering evidence of the fragility of relationships and the perfidy of men. In short, Christina Rossetti was not a complete stranger to love or, more accurately, to its betrayals and disappointments.

In the later years of Christina Rossetti's life, the religious devotion that had twice excused her from marriage became her dominant interest. Aside from William Michael's marriage in 1874, the most noteworthy events in her increasingly cloistered existence were the deaths of family members—Maria's in 1876, Dante Gabriel's in 1882, Mrs. Rossetti's in 1886—and her own illnesses. In 1871, Christina was struck with a serious thyroid disease that weakened her constitution for the rest of her life. While she did not remain an invalid after the worst ravages of the disease had spent themselves, her weakened condition moved her to constrict still further the narrowing circle of her life. In 1892, she underwent an operation for cancer, but the disease reappeared in 1893. She died of cancer in London on December 29, 1894, at the age of sixty-four.

Christina Rossetti's life was a rare combination of the extraordinary and the conventional, and the tension between the two strands was both energizing and exhausting. In some ways, she conformed to the stereotype of the Victorian woman: shy, self-effacing, unworldly, devoted to her family, to good works, and to God. Yet in her choice of profession she contradicted every Victorian dictum about female behavior: here was a woman who rejected the substance and the trappings, the restrictions and the securities of marriage—the only truly acceptable "vocation" for Victorian women—in favor of the singular insecurities and gratifications of the traditionally male vocation of poet.

The contradiction between these two facets of Rossetti's life—the traditional and the extraordinary—is nowhere more apparent than in her self-image. On the one hand, as a woman in Victorian England, she identified herself with her society's constricting definition of women. Many of Rossetti's remarks on this subject are well known. The following is certainly representative: When confused about how to manage her income tax form of 1888, she wrote to William Michael, "Vainly too have I declared myself a woman and not a man. Weakest minded of my sex I am only too glad to betake myself to you for rescue. Please, if you can, somehow convince some one of my having paid what I owed and being a transparently blameless victim." The language here is that of a woman who sees herself primarily as object, rejecting any responsibility for self-activation and control. William Michael seems to have accepted his sister's self-portrait; in a memoir of Christina Rossetti, he wrote, "She was one of the last persons with whom any one would feel inspirited to take a liberty, though one might, without any sort of remonstrance, treat her as the least important of womankind." [6]

But when referring to herself as poet, Rossetti projected a very different image. Willing to submit to William Michael's greater expertise in financial matters, she was nowhere near as self-deprecating and conciliatory about her writing. Although Dante Gabriel contributed to her professional development, particularly in compiling and publishing her volumes of poetry, Christina brooked little intervention—by him or anyone else—into the poetry itself. Defending her poem "The Prince's Progress" (1865) against Dante Gabriel's criticism and suggestions, she wrote archly that her "actual *Prince* seems to me invested with a certain artistic congruity of construction not lightly to be despised. . . . See how the subtle elements balance each other, and fuse into a noble conglom!" [7] While in this and many similar passages Christina Rossetti is diplomatic and gentle, she is also decisive and confident about the integrity of her art.

6. Packer, *Christina Rossetti,* 376–77; William Michael Rossetti (ed.), *The Poetical Works of Christina Georgina Rossetti* (London, 1904), "Memoir," ix.

7. William Michael Rossetti (ed.), *Rossetti Papers, 1862 to 1870* (New York, 1903), 77–78.

This contradictory self-image informs the life and work of Christina Rossetti and provides grounds for timidity and courage, abnegation and gratification, self-condemnation and self-love. In many areas of her life, she followed the female behavior prescribed by Victorian society, but it is to our decided benefit that she chose the act of writing poetry and the vocation of poet as the means of rejecting the script her society had prepared for her. Her choice made her not "redundant"[8] but rare.

The critical estimate of Christina Rossetti's poetry has been inconsistent since her death. During her lifetime, Rossetti always enjoyed great popular success; for the most part, she was also well received by the critics. Particularly outspoken in their praise were her contemporary artists— many of whom she never met. Sir Walter Alexander Raleigh, for example, proclaimed her "the best poet alive," and she was lauded by Coventry Patmore and by Swinburne, who dubbed her "the Jael who led their [the Pre-Raphaelites'] host to victory." Gerard Manley Hopkins was so inspired by her "Convent Threshold" that he composed a poetical reply— "A Voice from the World: Fragments of an Answer to Miss Rossetti's Convent Threshold." Impressed by her innovative technical skill, he used her poetry as a model for his own verse. At the time of the 1893 publication of *Verses,* she was acclaimed as "one of the greatest living poets" and one of "the foremost poets of the age."[9]

Alexander Macmillan, Christina Rossetti's publisher during most of her career, once said of her, "She is a true artist and will live."[10] Up to a few years ago, it looked as though Macmillan's prophecy had surely failed; for while the poetry (or a minute fraction of it) has survived in English literature anthologies, it has not flourished. Traditionally, anthologies of English and Victorian poetry have included only a very small percentage of her poetry, although in the last twenty years, the selections have increased. The second edition of the Houghton and Stange *Victorian Poetry and Poetics* (1968) contains seventeen Christina Rossetti poems while the first edition contained none. There are no Christina Rossetti poems included in the third edition of the *Norton Anthology of English*

8.   William Rathbone Greg, *Literary and Social Judgments* (Boston, 1873), 276.

9.   Ford Madox Hueffer, "The Collected Poems of Christina Rossetti," *Fortnightly Review,* o. s., LXXXI (1904), 393; Lionel Stevenson, *The Pre-Raphaelite Poets* (Chapel Hill, 1972), 107; Packer, *Christina Rossetti,* 391.

10.   Packer, *Christina Rossetti,* 309.

Literature, but ten are included in the fourth edition and eighteen in the fifth. Not until 1979 and R. W. Crump's first volume of *The Complete Poems of Christina Rossetti* was there a reliable edition of the poetry to replace William Michael Rossetti's (long out of print) 1904 *Poetical Works of Christina Georgina Rossetti.* (The second volume of Crump's edition appeared in 1986.) Nor is there an adequate collection of Rossetti's letters or an entirely satisfactory biography. As William Fredeman has noted, until 1963 the biographies were "incrementally repetitive, depending almost exclusively for their documentation on Mackenzie Bell, W. M. Rossetti, or one another."[11] Lona Mosk Packer's *Christina Rossetti* is the most complete biography, containing a number of previously unpublished or subsequently revised poems, but its ill-taken major thesis hopelessly distorts the image of Christina Rossetti both as a woman and as a poet. Until recently, Rossetti's work has received little attention from critics. Until 1986, only one full-length critical study of the poetry had been written, and it was limited in compass.[12]

In the late 1970s, a period of renewed critical interest in Rossetti's poetry began. This interest comes largely, though not entirely, from feminist critics. Sandra Gilbert and Susan Gubar's chapter on Rossetti in *The Madwoman in the Attic* and Dolores Rosenblum's essay in *Shakespeare's Sisters* were groundbreaking examples of the profitability of studying Rossetti's poetry in terms of what it meant to be female in Victorian England.[13] Since 1979, a number of articles have demonstrated further the happy combination of Rossetti's poetry and feminist criticism.[14] In recent years, Rossetti's "Devotional Poetry" (a rather un-

11.   William E. Fredeman, "The Pre-Raphaelites," in Frederic E. Faverty (ed.), *The Victorian Poets: A Guide to Research* (2nd ed.; Cambridge, Mass., 1968), 288.

12.   Thomas Burnett Swann, *Wonder and Whimsey: The Fantastic World of Christina Rossetti* (Francestown, N.H., 1960); Dolores Rosenblum, *Christina Rossetti: The Poetry of Endurance* (Carbondale, Ill., 1986): Antony H. Harrison, *Christina Rossetti in Context* (Chapel Hill, 1988) appeared while this book was in press.

13.   Sandra M. Gilbert and Susan Gubar, *The Madwoman in the Attic: The Woman Writer and the Nineteenth Century Literary Imagination* (New Haven, 1979); Dolores Rosenblum, "Christina Rossetti: The Inward Pose," in Sandra M. Gilbert and Susan Gubar (eds.), *Shakespeare's Sisters: Feminist Essays on Women Poets* (Bloomington, Ind., 1979), 82–98.

14.   See, for example, Dorothy Mermin, "Heroic Sisterhood in 'Goblin Market,' " *Victorian Poetry,* XXI (1983), 107–18; Helena Michie, "The Battle for Sisterhood:

satisfactory heading coined by William Michael Rossetti in his 1904 edition of his sister's poems) has received some important attention,[15] but interest in these poems still lags behind that paid to the love poems. On the whole, Rossetti scholarship is still undeveloped: there is room and need for more work on the devotional poems and the children's poems, for a complete edition of the letters and the prose works, for studies of derivation and influence, and for textual analyses. A productive but as-yet-untapped vein of Rossetti studies is the mutual indebtedness of Christina and Dante Gabriel Rossetti. While their lives were strikingly dissimilar, their poetic interests were often surprisingly congruent. The reputation of Christina's poetry would not suffer from being closely compared with her brother's work.

Regardless of whether we put her in the ranks of first- or second-class poets, Christina Rossetti has been the object of far less critical attention than have been her contemporaries of either class. Two recent articles on Rossetti, however, have accorded her a high position. In "Christina Rossetti: Poet," Joan Rees criticizes those approaches that deny "Christina Rossetti the long-overdue recognition which her skills and achievement as a poet deserve." According to Rees, Rossetti was "at her best a powerful, distinctive and highly skillful poet." And G. B. Tennyson writes, "Serious status . . . [is] accorded Christina Rossetti, with opinion probably equally divided as to whether she is a poet of the first or second rank."[16]

Contemplating the explanations for Rossetti's relative obscurity can be illuminating. One wonders if her reputation in literary history would be higher than it is if she had not been the sister of Dante Gabriel Rossetti. During their lifetimes, Christina unquestionably sat in her brother's shadow. As was the rule in Victorian families, the Rossetti brothers, not Christina and Maria, received formal education outside the home. When

Christina Rossetti's Strategies for Control in Her Sister Poems," *Journal of Pre-Raphaelite Studies*, III (1983), 38–55; and Miriam Sagan, "Christina Rossetti's 'Goblin Market' and Feminist Literary Criticism," *Pre-Raphaelite Review*, III (1980), 66–76.

15. McGann, "The Religious Poetry of Christina Rossetti"; John O. Waller, "Christ's Second Coming: Christina Rossetti and the Premillennialist William Dodsworth," *Bulletin of the New York Public Library*, LXXIII (1969), 465–82.

16. Joan Rees, "Christina Rossetti: Poet," *Critical Quarterly*, XXVI (1984), 59–72; G. B. Tennyson, *Victorian Devotional Poetry: The Tractarian Mode* (Cambridge, Mass., 1980), 198.

Gabriele Rossetti became ill in 1843, it was Dante Gabriel alone whose talents were deemed considerable enough to exempt him from joining the rest of the family in finding remunerative work. Only through her own eventual and rather mysterious illness could Christina claim the same exemption. As we have seen, she was also ineligible to participate in Dante Gabriel's Pre-Raphaelite Brotherhood, though she was without question among the most talented poets of the group. And in her own career as poet, she constantly received advice, guidance, and direction from her brother, much of which she managed to reject, not without some difficulty, as this letter from Christina to Dante Gabriel suggests:

I have thickened my skin and toughened the glass of my house sufficiently to bear some fraternal stone-throwing. Let us resume our subject [discussion of DGR's suggestions for revising her poem "Mirrors of Life and Death"]—& if possible finish it off.

Stanzas 1,2, shall very willingly & with hearty concurrence change places. My mouse and my mole [symbols which DGR objected to] I incline to cling to, on grounds that seem to me of some weight. Still, if you will let me have "Mirrors" back, I will consider my point before deciding. For really I think I might just as well have it & the rest back, & transact what little business remains to be done straight with the *Athenaeum,* instead of troubling you.[17]

The remarkable mix of defensiveness, diplomacy, and determination apparent in this letter was typical of the general posture Christina adopted toward her brother.

Contributing to what must have been a competitive relationship was occasional public confusion about the reputation of the two poets during their lifetimes. In a poetry collection entitled *Flower-Lore,* the author of Christina's "When I am dead, my dearest" was identified as Christina Gabriela Rossetti. That Christina herself was accustomed to compare her work unfavorably with Dante Gabriel's is evident in the rather pathetic (though possibly disingenuous) remark she once wrote to F. S. Ellis: "We are not all D.G.R.'s."[18]

Until very recently, this estimate had been accepted by literary histo-

17.   William Michael Rossetti (ed.), *The Family Letters of Christina Georgina Rossetti* (London, 1908), 66.

18.   Gisela Hönnighausen, "Emblematic Tendencies in the Works of Christina Rossetti," *Victorian Poetry,* X (1972), 10–11*n;* Lona Mosk Packer (ed.), *The Rossetti-Macmillan Letters* (Berkeley, 1963), 90.

rians, maybe for no other reason than custom. But within the past few years some of Dante Gabriel's most unjustified critical pronouncements on his sister's poetry have been challenged by Christina Rossetti scholars. His remark that Christina's "The Lowest Room" suffered from "a falsetto muscularity"[19] has been often quoted but rarely recognized as the benighted and misleading remark it is.[20] It has been discouraging for those interested in Christina Rossetti scholarship to check the Rossetti heading in the annual *MLA Bibliography;* year after year, publications on Dante Gabriel have exceeded those on Christina. In 1971, there were seventeen entries under Dante Gabriel's name, three under Christina's; in 1975, there were nine under Dante Gabriel's, one under Christina's; in 1980, encouragingly, there were two more entries (three of which were dissertations) under Christina's than under Dante Gabriel's; and in 1986, there were five for Dante Gabriel and four for Christina.

Undoubtedly, one reason for the relative lack of interest in Christina Rossetti has been the limited subject matter of her poetry. As one critic wrote, "Christina has not the scope, the depth, the variety of a truly great writer." In the same vein, B. Ifor Evans claimed, "The ubiquity of a single theme has often been suggested as the most limiting factor in Christina Rossetti's poetical work."[21] Christina herself was aware of her poetry's limited scope. In a letter to Dante Gabriel of April, 1870, she wrote, "It is not in me, and therefore it will never come out of me, to turn to politics or philanthropy with Mrs. Browning: such many-sidedness I leave to a greater than I, and having said my say, may well sit silent."[22]

Throughout the century, Christina Rossetti has been the kind of poet about whom critics can make easy, summarizing conclusions such as Christina Rossetti is a poet of loss or betrayal or denial or conflict. The problem with such pronouncements is not so much that they are inaccurate or even limited (which they surely are) but that they imply an equiv-

19. Oswald Doughty and John Robert Wahl (eds.), *Letters of Dante Gabriel Rossetti* (Oxford, 1967), III, 1380.

20. Mermin, "Heroic Sisterhood in 'Goblin Market,'" 115.

21. Elizabeth Jennings (ed.), *A Choice of Christina Rossetti's Verse* (London, 1970), 12; B. Ifor Evans, *English Poetry in the Later Nineteenth Century* (2nd ed.; New York, 1966), 90.

22. William Michael Rossetti (ed.), *The Family Letters of Christina Georgina Rossetti,* 31.

alence between narrowness of subject matter and narrowness of treatment. Christina Rossetti is surely a very personal poet (a more accurate
adjective than "limited" or "narrow"), but there are variety and constant
experimentation in her poetic renderings and resolutions of the personal
issues that so concerned her. While earlier critics objected to stylistic and
thematic repetitiveness, modern Rossetti scholars are beginning to realize
that her "restricted lexicon . . . repetitive formulations . . . [and] limited
metaphorical invention" operate not as liabilities but as unique assets,
offering her "the means to compose a distinctive self as woman and
poet."[23]

According to Jerome McGann, the reason Christina Rossetti has been
virtually ignored during much of the twentieth century is the highly
personal, context-dependent nature of her poetry. In a compelling argument, McGann finds fault, not with these qualities of the poetry, but
rather with the New Critical theories that automatically and mistakenly
rejected any poetry requiring a biographical or historical gloss. As
McGann points out, full appreciation of Rossetti's devotional poetry requires "conscious investment in the peculiarities of its Christian orienta-
tion, in the social and historical particulars which feed and shape the
distinctive features of her work." That the poetry needs such an investment does not make it inferior or incomplete. Indeed, McGann concludes that poetry like Rossetti's, which continues to survive though
"conscious of . . . [its] own limitedness . . . is the ground of all we can
mean by 'transcendence.'"[24] The recent revival of interest in Christina
Rossetti's poetry is, in large part, a reflection of this kind of critical
attitude—an attitude that values and analyzes all those circumstances,
however personal and topical, that inform the finished product of the
poem.

Feminist critics, working from much the same critical premise, but
with an emphasis on the crucial influence of gender on women writers,
are demonstrating the value of rejoining Christina Rossetti's poetry with
her life—just as McGann, Waller, and other critics have begun to repair
the seam between the poetry and its religious context. In both instances,
a remarkable reversal of the traditional attitude toward Rossetti is taking

23. Dolores Rosenblum, "Christina Rossetti's Poetry: Watching, Looking, Keeping Vigil," *Victorian Poetry,* XX (1982), 35.
24. McGann, "The Religious Poetry of Christina Rossetti," 132–33, 142.

place. The contextuality—historical, biographical, sexual, and religious—that earlier in the century was seen as limiting Rossetti's work is now being restored and restudied, offering a rich revision of Rossetti's art. What was once seen as narrow is beginning to look surprisingly capacious; what was once deemed personal and parochial is now called transcendent.

Close attention to Christina Rossetti's poetry—to its context and to its artistry—makes further underestimates of its achievement unlikely. Through a careful analysis of her contemporary setting and her artistic ability, Christina Rossetti emerges as a unique and important contributor to Victorian letters, whose often unconventional vision can be disguised by a decorous and reserved voice, and whose remarkably unified canon is belied by an apparent division between secular and religious concerns. Christina Rossetti's poetry is neither coy nor intentionally deceptive, but because of the social environment within which it was composed, it often resorts to indirection and understatement to tell sometimes startling truths. A serious and respectful examination of Rossetti's method can reveal much about the unrecognized integrity, courage, and intelligence of Christina Rossetti's art.

TWO

Widening the Narrow Way

t has become a biographical and critical commonplace to represent Christina Rossetti's life and work as fields of strenuous conflict. The accepted biographical view is that of a woman tormented by the opposition between her instinctive love of the pleasures of this world and a simultaneous conviction of the vanity and sinfulness of such an attachment. William Michael Rossetti, Mackenzie Bell, Mary Sandars, C. M. Bowra, Lona Mosk Packer, and, more recently, Sandra Gilbert and Susan Gubar have all portrayed Christina Rossetti's life as a painful struggle to subvert and repress her strong love of this world. The image is that of a rigorously self-denying woman who gradually learned to replace her need for immediate pleasures with the anticipation of the eternal delights of Heaven. In his "Memoir" included in the 1904 *Poetical Works of Christina Rossetti,* William Michael Rossetti describes his sister as "replete with the spirit of self-postponement, which passed into self-sacrifice whenever that quality was in demand. . . . The narrow path was the only one for her, and a lion in the same path made no difference." Mary Sandars subscribes to the same view in her 1930 biography: "Christina Rossetti's life . . . was one of inhibitions, her fullness had its root in self-denial, she cut off ruthlessly any desire or passion which might lead her out of the narrow way which seemed to her the right way." A persistent theme of Lona Mosk Packer's biography is that Christina Rossetti was a woman "at strife with herself." In his reminiscence of Christina Rossetti, Ford Madox Ford described her as "the tranquil Religious . . . undergoing within herself always a fierce struggle between the pagan desire for life, the light of the sun and love, and an asceticism that, in its almost more than Calvinistic restraint, reached also a point of frenzy." And Gilbert and Gubar write, "As a representative female poet-speaker, moreover, Rossetti believes she must learn to sing selflessly, despite pain, rather than selfishly, in celebration of pleasure." Virginia Woolf, who admired Rossetti's poetry, recognized how this personal conflict was reflected in Rossetti's poetic style: "Your eye observed with a sensual pre-Raphaelite intensity that must have surprised Christina the Anglo-Catholic. . . . [T]he pressure of a tremendous faith circles and clamps together these little songs. . . . No sooner have you feasted on beauty with your eyes than your mind tells you that beauty is vain and beauty passes."[1]

The accepted portrait of Christina Rossetti as a reluctantly self-denying ascetic is by no means groundless. Her reading and her religious inclinations in her youth reflected her attraction to rigorous self-denial and otherworldliness. From an early age, she was influenced by her thorough knowledge of the Bible, including its repeated lesson of *vanitas vanitatum*, and by *The Confessions of St. Augustine* and the *Imitation of Christ* by Thomas À Kempis. According to Eleanor Thomas, "The struggles and ideals of the fourth-century bishop and the medieval saint were echoed in her [Rossetti's] life and character. . . . In the *Imitation* Christina . . . was admonished to keep purpose with courage, to learn to be obedient, and as being earth and clay, to humble herself."[2] Anglo-Catholicism, to which Christina, Maria, Mrs. Rossetti, and, briefly, Dante Gabriel turned, insisted upon self-restraint and inner discipline. That a young girl as passionate and self-expressive as Christina should have devoted herself so thoroughly to a religion characterized by discipline, moderation, and emotional suppression is certainly evidence that she knew herself to be in need of some method of self-control.

While not without justification, the traditional representation of Christina Rossetti's self-depriving rejection of worldly pleasures is incomplete and simplistic; to accept this view is to oversimplify Rossetti's

---

1. William Michael Rossetti (ed.), *Poetical Works of Christina Georgina Rossetti*, "Memoir," lxvii; Mary F. Sandars, *The Life of Christina Rossetti* (London, 1930), 17; Packer, *Christina Rossetti*, 86; Ford Madox Ford, *Memories and Impressions: A Study in Atmospheres* (New York, 1911), 67; Gilbert and Gubar, *The Madwoman in the Attic*, 571; Virginia Woolf, *Common Reader: Second Series* (London, 1932), 242–43.

2. Eleanor Walter Thomas, *Christina Georgina Rossetti* (New York, 1931), 34.

attitudes toward life, religion, and poetry. Many of the poems written from 1848 to 1860 (between Rossetti's eighteenth and thirtieth years) do not support this tradition, but require us to review and revise our understanding of the mind and imagination behind the poetry.

As so many of the early poems demonstrate, Rossetti's attitude toward the world was complex; her "renunciation" of it reflects more than religious influence and more than masochistic repression, though elements of both are involved. Her rejection of the world was also based largely on a profound dissatisfaction with her life. The early poems present a young woman, constantly disappointed and frustrated, who gradually comes to renounce her life, not so much because she perceives it as inherently sinful, but because she finds it pallid, restrictive, and obstructive of her own potential. In the poems of this period, we see both a representation of this view of the world and a continuing examination of the reagents that might render the conditions of life acceptable, transmute them in such a way that her experience could satisfy her desires.

Throughout her career, Christina Rossetti examines the transforming potential of romantic love, art, and religion. During this first period of her career, romantic love and art receive primary attention. As so many of the love poems of this period demonstrate, Rossetti ultimately rejects realized romantic love as a re-former of experience, primarily because it is illusory and transient. But contemporaneous with her investigation of love is a probing examination of art and artistic creativity as possible cures for her dissatisfaction and disaffection. The act of writing poetry and the condition of being a poet become for Christina Rossetti the process for resolving her difficulties and an important, though not perfect, resolution itself.

One of the clearest and most extended statements of dissatisfaction with the world is the 1856 poem "The Lowest Room." Here, and in other related poems of the period, the dominant voice is not that of a timorous ascetic but that of a woman craving a total satisfaction not presently available to her. The speaker of this 280-line poem primarily recounts a conversation with her younger sister that occurred twenty years earlier. In that conversation, the speaker—then a young, unmarried woman—complains of the difference between the banality of her time and the heroism of the Homeric age. The younger sister, unmarried but engaged, takes issue with the speaker's disaffection from the present age and her romanticization of Homer's, finally silencing her with a reminder that one's relationship with Christ can make any life great. In the final thirteen stanzas, the speaker summarizes the twenty years following this conversation: the younger sister has married happily, had a daughter, and has devoted her life to her family and her religion; the speaker has lived alone, painfully trying to learn contentment and humility, to accept her allotted "lowest place, / The place assigned me here."

The movement of the poem is impelled by the diametric opposition between the two sisters. Although "nestling of the selfsame nest," the sisters are different in character, attitude, interests, and goals. According to the speaker, the younger sister is gentle, quiet, and forbearing, a seamless combination of feminine and Christian virtues. Throughout the poem, she is motivated by love—of her sister, of her lover (eventually her husband), and, most important, of Christ. The speaker is far less conventional and accepting than is her sister. A poetic version of Maggie Tulliver, the speaker is bright, searching, imaginative, and unhappy. In her relationship with her sister, she has clearly played the traditional male role while her sister has been thoroughly feminine:

> For mild she [the younger sister] was, of few soft words,
> > Most gentle, easy to be led,
> > Content to listen when I spoke
> > And reverence what I said.[3]

During the course of the conversation, the younger sister engages in the domestic activities of embroidering and gardening while the speaker appraises Homer's time and puzzles over the meaning of life.

One of the chief sources of the speaker's dissatisfaction is the behavior expected of her as a woman. While envious of her sister's unquestioning contentment, she continually reveals her own unsuitability for a life of quiet domesticity. To the speaker, such a life is "aimless"; its tasks, like her sister's sewing ("those holes / Amid that waste of white"), are meaningless, a "fritter[ing] away" of "blank life." At the end of the poem, she admires her sister's devotion to family life but expresses no regret at the different direction her own life has taken:

3. R. W. Crump (ed.), *The Complete Works of Christina Rossetti: A Variorum Edition* (2 vols. to date, Baton Rouge, 1979, 1986), I, 204. Subsequent citations of this multi-volume work will be abbreviated and take the following form: C,I:204.

While I? I sat alone and watched;
My lot in life, to live alone
In mine own world of interests,
Much felt but little shown.

(C, I: 207)

The tone here is not pained or regretful; it reflects what the speaker has implied all along—that she is not naturally suited for the traditional female role.

Accompanying this frustration with ill-fitting sex roles is a more general impatience with the pallor and vapidity of modern times. The speaker longs to live in a world like Homer's, when

"Men were men of might and right,
    Sheer might, at least, and weighty swords;
Then men in open blood and fire
    Bore witness to their words,
. . . .
"Calm in the utmost stress of doom,
    Devout toward adverse powers above,
They hated with intenser hate
    And loved with fuller love."

(C, I: 201)

She longs not only for the heroism and boldness of Homer's times but also for Homer's ability to create such worlds, his power to achieve a dramatic effect:

"He stirs my sluggish pulse like wine,
    He melts me like the wind of spice,
Strong as strong Ajax' red right hand,
    And grand like Juno's eyes.
. . . .
I cannot fire and tempest-toss:—
Besides, those days were golden days,
    Whilst these are days of dross."

(C, I: 200–201)

Here, it is the poet's power she longs for—the power to create, transform, and influence. An implicit irony of the poem is that the younger sister, whom the speaker admires but never tries to emulate, possesses similar power. Through her sewing, her flower gathering (she "ranged them with instinctive taste / Which all my books had failed to teach"), and her daughter ("Fair image of her own fair youth"), she too is productive and creative. And in her gentle chastisement of the speaker's pagan tendencies, she wields tremendous influence: the speaker spends the next twenty years trying to follow her sister's advice.

> Not to be first: how hard to learn
>   That lifelong lesson of the past;
> Line graven on line and stroke on stroke;
>   But, thank God, learned at last.

> (C, I: 207)

But the speaker has not learned to curb her ambition as well as she would like us to believe. Although she says she has learned to be "Content to take the lowest place, / The place assigned me here"—learned, that is, to be patient and humble—the final two stanzas of the poem discredit her posture of self-immolating resignation:

> Yet sometimes, when I feel my strength
>   Most weak, and life most burdensome,
> I lift mine eyes up to the hills
>   From whence my help shall come:

> Yea, sometimes still I lift my heart
>   To the Archangelic trumpet-burst,
> When all deep secrets shall be shown,
>   And many last be first.

> (C, I: 207)

Her passion for excellence and superiority is alive; she has merely turned her attention from the irretrievable glories of Homer to the still-remote but, to a devout Christian, more attainable, future glories of Heaven. She continues to crave more beauty, knowledge, and excellence than her *mortal* life can offer. While the years may have softened her, the speaker has not really compromised; having rejected the conventional female goals of marriage and family, she sustains a passionate ambition for knowledge ("When all deep secrets shall be shown") and excellence.

According to William Michael Rossetti, the final thirteen stanzas of the poem represent growth and development on the part of the speaker. In discussing his brother's objections to the "falsetto muscularity" of this poem, William Michael wrote, "The real gist of *The Lowest Room*—i.e. the final acceptance, by the supposed speaker, of a subordinate and be-dimmed position—is clearly the very reverse of 'falsetto muscularity.'"[4] Yet the speaker's "final acceptance" is more apparent than real. Although her concluding words are cloaked in biblical language (there are strong echoes of the Old and New Testaments throughout the poem), they reveal essentially the same attitude she expressed twenty years earlier—dissatis-faction with the "mean and cold and slow" conditions of her life and a yearning for "golden days."

This poem is not among the best that Rossetti wrote (though its natural, sustained dialogue is impressive), but it is important for repre-senting the dissatisfaction that plagues the speakers of this period, and for anticipating one of the solutions at which Christina Rossetti the poet will finally arrive: the seeking of satisfaction from remote, visionary worlds—both religious and artistic. "The Lowest Room" is also one of the first poems to contain the dense and ambiguous ending that Rossetti will master in her middle years. Here, as in "Goblin Market," "A Pause," and "Remember," what the speaker presents as a concluding resolution must be evaluated in terms of other implicit, but quietly powerful, elements of the poem.

Written eleven months after "The Lowest Room," "The Heart Know-eth Its Own Bitterness"[5] is another complaint about the inadequacies and limitations of experience. In the later poem, the speaker is primarily concerned with the seemingly inevitable limitations within human (par-ticularly romantic) relationships. She yearns for a relationship in which she can be intensely active *and* completely receptive.

> To give, to give, not to receive!
> I long to pour myself, my soul,
> Not to keep back or count or leave,
>   But king with king to give the whole.
> I long for one to stir my deep—
>   I have had enough of help and gift—
>   I long for one to search and sift
> Myself, to take myself and keep.[6]

4. William Michael Rossetti (ed.), *Poetical Works of Christina Georgina Rossetti,* "Notes," 461.

5. Christina Rossetti wrote another poem by this title in December, 1852.

6. William Michael Rossetti (ed.), *The Poetical Works of Christina Rossetti*

This passage is a curious combination of stereotypically male and female urges: she wants to be a generous king, pouring herself into another, and at the same time she wants to be the recipient of such action, to be taken, ravished. But such androgyny is unavailable to her in her current relationship, as is the sensual gratification that she craves. The speaker upbraids her unidentified and silent friend in revealing physical language:

> You scratch my surface with your pin,
>   You stroke me smooth with hushing breath:—
> Nay pierce, nay probe, nay dig within,
>   Probe my quick core and sound my depth.
>
> (R: 192)

Her frustration with the mildness and superficiality of her friend is one aspect of a wider sensual dissatisfaction. All her senses are hungering for a repletion unavailable in this world.

> Not in this world of hope deferred,
>   This world of perishable stuff:—
> Eye hath not seen nor ear hath heard
>   Nor heart conceived that full "enough."
>
> (R: 192–93)

In both this poem and "The Lowest Room," the speakers posit a solution for their polymorphous dissatisfaction. But here the vision of Heaven is presented, not as a solution for frustrated ambition as in "The Lowest Room," but specifically as an alternative to the problems of human relationships: "There [in Heaven] God shall join and no man part, / I full of Christ and Christ of me." The marriage the speaker envisions is not with her mortal lover but with Christ, through whom both her desire for repletion and for self-assertion will be satisfied. Equally important, in her relationship with Christ she will discover a way to erase the distance and the separateness that plague human relationships ("Here [in this life] moans the separating sea, / Here harvests fail, here breaks the heart"). The final line of the poem, "I full of Christ and Christ of me," expresses not only repletion but also union. In this line, it is impossible to tell where Christ leaves off and the speaker begins; both are active as well as passive; both are serving and being served. The relationship has gone beyond

(London, 1904), 192. Subsequent citations of this work will be abbreviated and take the following form: R:192.

perfect equality to a state of perfect union—the condition that will become the ultimate goal of the troubled speakers of many of Rossetti's later religious poems.

The religious overtones of this poem, as well as William Michael Rossetti's decision to include it among the "Devotional Poems" in the 1904 edition, obscure the fact that "The Heart Knoweth Its Own Bitterness" is as much a sociological statement as a religious one. Here and in "The Lowest Room," Rossetti presents the plight of every intelligent, passionate Victorian girl: the virtual impossibility of satisfying any ambitions and desires that went beyond the restrictively narrow bounds of acceptable feminine behavior, decorum, and good taste. The heavenly satiety that these speakers hunger for springs as much from what they were deprived of by society as it does from religious devotion. As "The Heart Knoweth Its Own Bitterness" and "The Lowest Room" make perfectly clear, Rossetti's society barred women from sexual satisfaction, intellectual stimulation, and purposeful, active creativity. These and related poems are actually thinly disguised indictments of society, indicating just how oppressive Rossetti found the conditions she was born to. Within the conventional religious conclusions of these poems, Rossetti has hidden a set of desires and ambitions forbidden by her society.

It is not only social restrictions that frustrate the speakers of the early poems. Another disappointment is the impermanence of earthly beauty. Highly appreciative of the beauties of nature, these speakers are tormented by natural decay and death. In the late 1850s and early 1860s, Christina Rossetti becomes virtually obsessed with this natural law. As she writes in "Spring" (August 17, 1859), she cannot find complete pleasure in the beauties of nature because she cannot repress her knowledge of their imminent decay:

> There is no time like Spring,
> Like Spring that passes by;
> There is no life like Spring-life born to die,—
> . . . .
> There is no time like Spring that passes by,
> Now newly born, and now
> Hastening to die.
>
> (C, I: 35)

In these poems of foreboding, Rossetti is objecting to more than the impermanence of natural beauty: she is mourning the mortal condition, searching, as in "June" (1863), for a way to stop time.

> If the year would stand
> Still at June for ever,
> With no further growth on land
> Nor further flow of river,
> If all nights were shortest nights
> And longest days were all the seven.
> This might be a merrier world
> To my mind to live in.

(R: 354)

At the same time that Rossetti was writing poems of complaint about the feebleness and inadequacy of her times and of human relationships, she was experimenting in other poems with the possibility of romantic love as an answer to her speakers' frustration and dissatisfaction. In these poems, a number of young women attempt to cure their ennui by entering into sexual liaisons that eventually become disastrous. Many of the love poems written in Rossetti's late teens and twenties repeat the same sequence: A young woman with high expectations about the magic of love yearns for change and romantic involvement; she enters a relationship with a man, soon discovering the dangers of the involvement; sometimes she is able to escape the relationship and return gratefully to her initial situation, but more frequently she must submit to a ghastly continuance of the relationship. It is not the sexual nature of these relationships that threatens these speakers, but rather the permanence and the abdication of individuality that Rossetti saw as inherent in all such liaisons.

Among the earliest examples of this sequence is the 1847 poem "Repining." The speaker's situation at the opening of the poem is similar to that of the elder sister in "The Lowest Room"; she, like Tennyson's Mariana, is weary of the dullness and solitude of her domestic lot and longs for human involvement and love:

> She sat alway through the long day
> Spinning the weary thread away;
> And ever said in undertone,
> "Come, that I be no more alone."
> . . . .

Day followed day and still she sighed
For love, and was not satisfied.

(R: 9)

Unlike the sister in "The Lowest Room," the speaker in "Repining" has her wishes granted. Late one night while in bed, she is approached by a mysterious and romantic male figure who offers to give her the experience she craves, to show her the world that she has longed to be a part of. But the sights soon change her longing to fear and horror: in rapid succession she sees an avalanche, an overwhelming sea storm, a gigantic fire, and a bloody war. The speaker's dream of "dear communion without strife" turns into a nightmare of death and destruction. More telling is the association between her romantic guide and the experiences he reveals to her. As the speaker realizes, "Where'er we go it [death] followeth." This poem is the first of many renderings of the lesson that relationships can be dangerous; like the cataclysmic acts witnessed by the speaker, they can annihilate the individual. In the face of this realization, the speaker of this poem chooses to return to her life of solitude and innocence: "My heart's prayer [of experiencing life and love] putteth me to shame; / Let me return to whence I came." Unlike the denser "Lowest Room," this poem is a fairly simple cautionary tale; the speaker does learn a lesson through her experience and happily returns to her earlier life. What makes "Repining" important is its association of a realized dream of love—a love that the speaker had hoped would solve her problems—with death and destruction.

The reason Christina Rossetti looked to romantic love as a way to ease the frustrations and dissatisfactions of her speakers is more complicated than it might seem. If we read the related poems of this period carefully, we see that love is sought, not only as a cure for loneliness and frustration, but also, and more important, as a powerful agent for *transforming* experience. Most of these speakers want more than companionship and passion—they, like the elder sister in "The Lowest Room," want a complete alteration of their existence. Although Rossetti herself did not have a wide experience of romantic relationships, she undoubtedly knew that the initial stages of love work like a painter's brush, changing the unexceptional into the wonderful. But as so many poems of this period demonstrate, love, with its transforming power, is finally an inadequate, even dangerous, solution. Unlike a painting, which, once finished, will not disappear, the glow cast by romantic love in its early stages often turns out to be both temporary and false. Once it dissipates, and in Rossetti's poetry it usually does, the underlying reality can be a blank and lifeless bondage to another person.

This pessimistic view of love was a fairly accurate reflection of the realities of Rossetti's time, when being courted and adored as a young woman had absolutely nothing to do with the reality of marriage, based as it was on a severe power imbalance between the sexes and impossibly re-strictive codes of behavior for women. As Jerome McGann remarks, Rossetti's own observations of the relationships in her immediate circle and in greater Victorian society must have contributed to her jaded view of relationships: "She clearly recognized that the patterns of such failure surrounded her everywhere, in art as well as life: in society at large . . . and near at hand, in her early home life as well as in the later, disastrous love experiences which centered on her brother Dante Gabriel."[7] The positive, transforming power that the Rossetti speakers look for in romantic love becomes in fact a corrupt, restricting power from which there is often no escape, just as for Rossetti's contemporaries there was no escape from marriage. This, finally, is the danger of love—that it can appear to be one thing and turn out to be quite another. That the dangers of realized love haunted Christina Rossetti during this period in her career is amply demonstrated by the many poems reiterating the association between love and death first made in "Repining." The speakers of these poems pine for romantic love, but once they find it, they are always sorry; their relationships become literally dis-illusioning. As the illusion—the transformation first created by the relationships—dispels, each speaker is locked into a situation far worse than that in which she was originally found.

Among the finest examples of this process of disillusionment is the hauntingly lovely "Moonshine" (June, 1852). A provocatively simple ballad about a young woman's first experience with love, "Moonshine" is similar to "Repining" in situation. In "Moonshine," a man entreats a maiden to accompany him on a long journey. She agrees, only to find that the journey is not what she had expected. While in "Repining" the speaker gives us much information about her state of mind before and during her adventure, we

7. Jerome J. McGann, "Christina Rossetti's Poems: A New Edition and a Re-valuation," *Victorian Studies,* XXIII (1980), 241.

have almost no such understanding of the young woman of "Moonshine," who is not the speaker of the poem. In fact, neither of the two characters of "Moonshine" is developed in any way; they appear merely as representations of man and woman. The final effect of the poem is all the more chilling for this suggestion of the universality of the woman's predicament.

The initial setting of "Moonshine" is one of beauty and harmony. In the first stanza, Rossetti presents what the reader will learn to recognize as desirable conditions: daylight, warmth, and natural beauty.

> Fair the sun riseth,
>   Bright as bright can be,
> Fair the sun shineth
>   On a fair fair sea.
>
> (R: 150)

The gradual disappearance of sunlight through the course of the poem becomes a measure of the corruption or distortion of the young woman's experience within her marriage. That her relationship with the sailor is a kind of marriage is made clear in stanzas 2 through 4. In the second stanza, the man proposes to the maiden (the only time he speaks during the poem), and in the third and fourth stanzas, she accepts his proposal on the condition that he promise her fidelity and protection.

> "Across the water
> Wilt thou come with me,
> Miles and long miles, love,
> Over the salt sea?"
>
> "If thou wilt hold me
> Truly by the hand,
>   I will go with thee
> Over sea and sand.
>
> "If thou wilt hold me
> That I shall not fall,
>   I will go with thee,
> Love, in spite of all."
>
> (R: 150)

The last words of the fourth stanza, "in spite of all," ominously suggest that the maiden accepts the proposal with some misgiving.

The initial stage of the relationship—before the journey is under way—seems auspicious; in fact, for a while, life is more beautiful than it has ever been:

> Fair the moon riseth
> On her heavenly way,
> Making the waters
> Fairer than by day.
>
> (R: 151)

But it is now the moon, not the sun, that is in ascendance, and though it seems that moonshine (like the relationship it accompanies) has transfiguring, beautifying power, the maiden soon learns to her sorrow that its power is the unreal, apparitional power of the "moonshine" of literary convention—a corrupt imitation of the more honest light of day. Once the man has guided "the vessel / From the water's edge," the brilliance of the moonlight begins to wane, robbing the relationship of its borrowed, and finally false, beauty.

> Fair the moon saileth
> With her pale fair light,
> Fair the girl gazeth
> Out into the night.
>
> Saith she, "Like silver
> Shines thy hair, not gold":
> Saith she, "I shiver
> In thy steady hold.
>
> "Love," she saith weeping,
> "Loose thy hold awhile;
> My heart is freezing
> In thy freezing smile."
>
> (R: 151)

With the dissipation of the illusion cast by romantic love, the young woman finds herself in a restraining, loveless relationship from which there is no escape. By this point, even the false light of the moon has disappeared, a disappearance that prefigures the woman's own death, or death-in-life.

> The moon is hidden
> By a silver cloud,
> Fair as a halo
> Or a maiden's shroud.
>
> (R: 151)

Without the transforming light of romantic love, actions that earlier in the poem had seemed innocent and positive take on an ominous, sinister quality, particularly as we know they will never stop, despite the woman's unhappiness.

> No more beseeching,
> Ever on they go:
> The vessel rocketh [see stanza 6]
> Softly to and fro:
> And still he holds her [see stanzas 4 and 8]
> That she shall not fall,
> Till pale mists whiten
> Dimly over all.
> . . . .
> Onward and onward,
> Ever hand in hand, [see stanza 3]
> From sun and moonlight
> To another land.
>
> (R: 151)

The conditions under which the maiden had accepted the man's offer—that he be faithful and protective—have turned into nightmarish conditions of bondage. When he continues to hold her in stanza 14 ("And still he holds her / That she shall not fall"), we realize that the woman is on the verge of falling, not because of her innocent fragility, as in stanza 4, but because of the sheer horror of her situation. The language remains the same, but its implications have changed drastically. We must conclude that love is an agent of transformation, but not of the kind Rossetti is looking for. Love has rendered the maiden's experience not more precious but more base. The alchemy has failed.

"Amor Mundi" (1865), essentially a religious allegory about traveling the road to Hell, makes its point through a situation that parallels those in "Repining" and "Moonshine": An attractive stranger invites a solitary woman on a journey that ultimately deteriorates into a nightmare. Repeated use of this dramatic vehicle testifies further to Rossetti's ambivalence toward long-term relationships between men and women. "Amor Mundi" begins with the woman questioning the man as he passes by her: "'O where are you going with your love-locks flowing, / On the west wind blowing along this valley track?'" Unlike the maiden in "Moonshine," who accepted the man's proposal primarily out of a need for protection, this woman decides out of curiosity to accompany the attractive stranger on his journey.

As in "Moonshine," the initial stage of the journey is pleasant and beautiful:

> So they two went together in glowing August weather,
>   The honey-breathing heather lay to their left and right;
> And dear she was to doat on, her swift feet seemed to float on
>   The air like soft twin pigeons too sportive to alight.
>
> (C, I: 214)

(The final two lines of this stanza must rank among the most charming and felicitously phrased of all Christina Rossetti's verse.) But soon, the journey is threatened:

> "Oh what is that in heaven where grey cloud-flakes are seven,
>   Where blackest clouds hang riven just at the rainy skirt?"
> "Oh that's a meteor sent us, a message dumb, portentous,
>   An undeciphered solemn signal of help or hurt."
>
> (C, I: 214)

Rossetti's treatment of the "message" is particularly interesting. The meteor is an equivocal symbol that neither the guide nor the woman interprets: it is dumb, yet portentous; it is either good or it is bad. (Rossetti did the same thing with "the silver cloud" in "Moonshine," which was "Fair as a halo / Or a maiden's shroud.") Presumably, if the woman in "Amor Mundi" knew how to interpret the meteor's message she could escape what becomes a disastrous experience. It is as much the woman's failure to choose the correct interpretation of the meteor—indeed, to choose any interpretation at all—as it is her incautious decision to accompany the mysterious stranger that brings about her tragedy. Here and in other poems, Rossetti is expressing a mistrust of symbols and of the many possible meanings that a single object may have. Like some of her American contemporaries (Melville and Hawthorne, for example), Rossetti was excited, but also disturbed, by the plurality of a symbol's interpretive possibilities. A sign with many possible meanings certainly enriches the life that to many of these speakers seems flat, but it also suggests more chaos in the universe than a woman with Rossetti's faith in a stable, decipherable moral system could tolerate. In many poems, Rossetti uses such a symbol or a wildly proliferating simile as a single symbol itself—a sign of the simultaneous dangers and attractions of an indecipherable poetic code.

Once the woman in "Amor Mundi" has failed to read the symbol, her fate is sealed. Although in the rest of the journey she encounters other portents, their messages are unambiguous. The "scaled and hooded worm," the "thin dead body which waits the eternal term" are unequivocal signs of death and decay. Their clearly limited reference emphasizes that the time for choice is gone, that the path the woman is traveling can only lead to Hell.

> "Turn again, O my sweetest,—turn again, false and fleetest:
>   This beaten way thou beatest I fear is hell's own track."
> "Nay, too steep for hill-mounting; nay, too late for cost-counting:
>   This downhill path is easy, but there's no turning back."
>
>   (C, I: 214)

"Amor Mundi" is reminiscent of "Moonshine" in theme and dramatic situation only. Stylistically, the two are worlds apart. While the cardinal feature of "Moonshine" is an incantatory simplicity of language and meter, the later poem is more technically demanding. The meter is iambic heptameter (not popular in English verse since the early seventeenth century), and though the end-rhyme pattern is unexceptional (*abab*), the recurring system of internal rhyme is complicated. In each stanza, the fifth and the final words of the first line rhyme with each other and with the fifth word of each stanza's second line. Similarly, the fifth word and final word (or final two words) of every third line rhyme. Furthermore, throughout the poem these internal rhymes are all feminine. Not once does the pattern break down, but not once does a word or rhyme sound forced or unlikely. The final effect of this scheme is an impression of easy and slippery celerity—an impression especially appropriate to a poem describing the downhill path to Hell. Setting up what appear to be impossibly rigorous technical demands is a characteristic feature of Rossetti's poetry. The brilliant "Passing Away" of 1860 (No. 3 of "Old and

New Year Ditties")—which Lionel Stevenson has called "a *tour de force* in monorhyme"—and "Downcast" of 1856 are further examples of the poet's fondness for, and success at, technically rigorous forms.[8]

During the first half of her career, Rossetti was fascinated by the demon-lover motif that characterizes "Moonshine" and "Amor Mundi." Instances of young women being transported to a condition of life-in-death by ghastly, sometimes ghostly, lovers occur in "Love from the North," "The Hour and the Ghost," "Jessie Cameron," and "A Coast-Nightmare." While these poems fit well both within a general balladic tradition and the Romantic tradition of such poems as Keats's "La Belle Dame Sans Merci," Rossetti's frequent reworking of the theme suggests a serious personal interest in the domination of women by mysterious, powerful male figures. In many of these poems, the woman is clearly attracted to the man but accompanies him against her will, unable to distinguish between attraction and repulsion, between choice and compulsion. One of the best statements of this ambivalence appears in "Love from the North" (1856), where a woman is carried away from her fiancé by a "strong man from the north":

> He took me in his strong white arms,
>   He bore me on his horse away
> O'er crag, morass, and hairbreadth pass,
>   But never asked me yea or nay.
>
> He made me fast with book and bell,
>   With links of love he makes me stay;
> Till now I've neither heart nor power
>   Nor will nor wish to say him nay.
>   (C, I: 30)

The woman is in much the same predicament as the woman in "Moonshine," except that here she seems to be truly attracted to the man, who offers her not fidelity and security but passion and magic. This "love from the north" actually does her a service by rescuing her from a marriage she did not want to make; he is, in fact, just the lover the speaker of "The Heart Knoweth Its Own Bitterness" despaired of finding. Yet he has so overpowered her that she cannot determine the extent of her own complicity in the relationship. She may have gained love (which was lacking in

8. Stevenson, *The Pre-Raphaelite Poets*, 105.

"Moonshine"), but it has cost her control of her own life; for that reason, Rossetti cannot present it positively.

In "Jessie Cameron" (1864), Rossetti creates a woman capable of saying no to a man who wants her, but the results are as disastrous as they are for the compliant women of "Moonshine" and "Amor Mundi." After resisting the repeated entreaties of her would-be lover, Jessie is mysteriously drowned, along with the persistent man. The suggestion is that the man, who had ominous connections ("Some say that he had gipsy blood. . . . Some say his grandam was a witch"), killed Jessie for refusing his proposals. For some of Rossetti's women, pride, independence, and outspokenness—as well as compliance and dependence—are liabilities.

Not every poem from this period portrays love and relationships as negatively as do the poems just discussed. In one of Rossetti's finest poems, "A Pause" (1853), love is presented as a potent and beautiful reforming force, although the ending of the poem seriously questions whether such a force has a place in this life. The action of the sonnet is reminiscent of "Moonshine," "Repining," and "Amor Mundi": A solitary woman, waiting for a man, finds herself transported to another world upon his arrival. But the woman's experience in "A Pause" is the exact opposite of her counterparts' in the other poems. In "A Pause," the waiting woman is on the verge of death, if not already dead. She waits for a man she has known and loved a long time, but of whose regard she is uncertain—not for an unknown man who can bring her protection or knowledge or experience.

> They made the chamber sweet with flowers and leaves,
>   And the bed sweet with flowers on which I lay;
>   While my soul, love-bound, loitered on its way.
> I did not hear the birds about the eaves,
> Nor hear the reapers talk among the sheaves:
>   Only my soul kept watch from day to day,
>   My thirsty soul kept watch for one away:—
> Perhaps he loves, I thought, remembers, grieves.
>
> (R: 308)

The woman has cut every tie to the mortal world but her connection to this man; she does not want to leave this life until she has some assurance of his love for her. Oblivious to the life around her ("I did not hear the birds about the eaves, / Nor hear the reapers talk among the sheaves"), she concentrates on her vigil: "Only my soul kept watch from day to day, / My thirsty soul kept watch for one away." When at last he does come, her watching, waiting soul senses his arrival with uncanny sensitivity: "At length there came the step upon the stair, / Upon the lock the old familiar hand."

Once assured of his presence and thus his love, the woman, in one of the finest Rossetti endings, turns the extreme sensitivity of her soul to the experience of being received into Heaven.

> Then first my spirit seemed to scent the air
> Of Paradise; then first the tardy sand
> Of time ran golden; and I felt my hair
> Put on a glory, and my soul expand.
>
> (R: 308)

If we were to read this poem in isolation from other poems of this period, we would probably see the relationship between the man and woman as a glorious thing; it is, after all, the man's love, as expressed by his presence at her deathbed, that transports the woman to Paradise. In an exact reversal of the concluding situation of "Moonshine" and "Amor Mundi," the relationship transports the speaker not to a state of death-in-life, but rather to life-in-death. But we must remember that however blessed the realm to which the speaker is removed, she goes there alone; she is not brought back to life by the man's presence to enjoy a happy relationship, nor are the two transported together to enjoy a heavenly union. The man has been a catalyst for the transformation of the woman's experience, but there will be no further relationship. Given the disillusionment of previous speakers with the power of love, Rossetti, in "A Pause," creates the perfect solution: love works its magical transformation, but the woman is immediately exempted from the disenchantment that inevitably follows. The sonnet actually conflates two remedies for the Rossetti speakers' great disappointment with life—the dangerous remedy of love and the remote remedy of eternal blessedness.

While Rossetti was exploring in her poetry the possibilities and the disappointments of romantic relationships, she was also paying more attention to an alternative agent of change and gratification: the act of writing poetry. During this period, Rossetti's poetry developed a self-conscious concern with the process and the product of this craft that had attracted her since childhood. Increasingly, the frustrated figure of the early poems finds a partial solution to her difficulties within the practice of poetry. The considerable body of poems in the Rossetti canon about poetry reveal Rossetti's realization that as a poet, a creative artist, she could allow her imagination to reshape experience to better suit her desires and expectations. Having found reality unacceptable, she realized that it was "better to dream," that is, live in imaginative worlds, "than wake," for "oh in waking / The sights are not so fair." As a poet, she could give form to her dreams of vivid experience, of permanent and intense beauty, but because they were only dreams, she would be freed from the threatening necessity of physically participating in them. With Elizabeth Barrett Browning, the speaker might admit:

> I lived with visions for my company
> Instead of men and women, years ago,
> And found them gentle mates, nor thought to know
> A sweeter music than they played to me.

But while the cloistered Elizabeth Barrett resorted to this habit out of necessity, Christina Rossetti adopted it quite willingly. In the role of artist she found justification for creating new imagined worlds that were more capable of satisfying her conflicting needs than was her actual world. Her artistic creations served her in the same way that Byron's served him:

> 'Tis to create, and in creating live
> A being more intense, that we endow
> With form our fancy, gaining as we give
> The life we image.[9]

Although "A Birthday" (1857) is explicitly a poem about love, it is also a remarkable statement of Rossetti's growing understanding of the power of art. One of the few joyful love poems in the canon, "A Birthday" documents the speaker's search for a medium that can accurately express her joy. In the first stanza, she turns to figurative language, attempting to find in nature correlatives for her strong emotions. Using original and well-developed imagery, Rossetti compares her happiness to three natural

9.   Elizabeth Barrett Browning, *Sonnets from the Portuguese,* in Harriet Waters Preston (ed.), *The Complete Poetical Works of Elizabeth Barrett Browning* (Boston, 1900), XXVI, 219; George Gordon, Lord Byron, *Childe Harold's Pilgrimage,* Canto III, in Paul E. More (ed.), *The Complete Poetical Works of Byron* (Boston, 1905), 36.

phenomena, only to conclude that these natural images are inadequate reflections:

> My heart is like a singing bird
>   Whose nest is in a watered shoot;
> My heart is like an apple tree
>   Whose boughs are bent with thickset fruit;
> My heart is like a rainbow shell
>   That paddles in a halcyon sea;
> My heart is gladder than all these
>   Because my love is come to me.
>
> (C, I: 36–37)

Leaving behind both the references to nature and the impulse to compare, the speaker adopts an entirely different strategy in stanza 2. No longer tentative and experimental, she demands that her happiness be put into action, be the stuff from which to fashion a permanent artifact.

> Raise me a dais of silk and down;
>   Hang it with vair and purple dyes;
> Carve it in doves and pomegranates,
>   And peacocks with a hundred eyes;
> Work it in gold and silver grapes,
>   In leaves and silver fleurs-de-lys;
> Because the birthday of my life
>   Is come, my love is come to me.
>
> (C, I: 37)

The similes of stanza 1, as well as the references to fleeting moments in nature, have disappeared; it is as if the speaker has realized that similes finally point out distance and dissimilarity, and that singing birds and rainbow shells are too fragile and temporary to represent her joy. Her love is so powerful that it calls for action ("Raise me a dias") as well as words, for permanent, not fleeting, versions of natural beauty. The speaker recognizes in stanza 2 that the more permanent the artifact—here, the construction of an elaborate dais carved with images of nature—the better it can express and immortalize her joy. It is important to realize that the speaker's demand in stanza 2 for a reformulation of her happiness is expressed through the poem itself. Simile has collapsed into metaphor, experimentation has given way to command, and impermanence has been replaced by stability, but all these changes have been made possible by, and occurred within, the poem itself. In "A Birthday," we see the power of poetry both to express strong feeling and to put it into more stable form. It is to these properties of poetry that Christina Rossetti is drawn throughout her career.

Just as the poetry that Christina Rossetti wrote could create better, more lasting worlds, the poetic vocation itself afforded her an important alternative to the constricting dependency and servitude imposed upon most Victorian women—whether they were wives, mothers, governesses, or shopgirls. Writing poetry offered both a fantastic and a real refuge from the troubling realities of Rossetti's existence. By choosing to become a poet, Rossetti literally did gain the life she imaged—a life exempt from the risks run by the troubled women speakers of such poems as "Moonshine" and "Repining," but with greater gratification than the insipid relationship complained of in "The Heart Knoweth Its Own Bitterness." In her career as poet, she found a role decidedly preferable to the obvious alternative of becoming a wife—a role for which, as both her poetry and her life demonstrate, she knew herself to be unsuited.

Through time, Rossetti's emotional investment in her vocation became enormous. Her decision to see herself as a serious, professional poet had clearly been made before 1853, the year she spent at Frome-Selwood with her mother and ailing father. William Michael Rossetti observed that while his sister did help with the school her mother started at Frome, her primary interest was her poetry. As he so delicately phrased it, "Still she was not at all unconscious of her poetic powers." The implications of this observation should be emphasized, for it suggests an overlooked aspect of Christina Rossetti's character. Devoted as she was to her family, she apparently chose to direct the majority of her energies, not to supporting her parents at a most difficult time, but to developing her beloved vocation. Whatever its motivations, such self-absorbed single-mindedness is remarkable in a woman traditionally characterized as "replete with the spirit of self-postponement, which passed into self-sacrifice whenever that quality was in demand."[10]

Christina Rossetti had begun writing poetry when she was about ten, but it was not until the late 1840s (about the time her grandfather printed,

10. William Michael Rossetti, *Some Reminiscences,* I, 109; William Michael Rossetti (ed.), *Poetical Works of Christina Georgina Rossetti,* "Memoir," lxvii.

on his private press, a collection of her verses) that her work began to demonstrate a serious concern with this crucial decision to become a dedicated professional poet. Some poems portray the poet's dedication to her chosen vocation; others, her ambivalence about the wisdom of her decision; and still others, her anguish about the sacrifices necessitated by that decision. Eugene Brzenk's contention that "poems celebrating dedication to art, poetry, and the life of the imagination are conspicuously absent from Christina Rossetti's poetry" is false; Rossetti was a dedicated and self-conscious artist whose poetry indicates a keen fascination with all the aspects of her craft—its power, its perquisites, its costs, its limitations.[11]

In her correspondence with her publishers, Rossetti frequently expressed concern about her public reputation. This "contemplative mystic"[12] asked both Macmillan and Ellis "whether my name is marketable." Regarding the publication of *Speaking Likenesses,* she wrote, "I only hope the public appetite [for the volume] will not be satisfied with 6 or 60, but crave on for 600 or 6000 at least!" A few months later, in January, 1875, she continued in the same vein: "I am pleased to hear of more than 1000 'Speaking Likenesses' having been disposed of: truth to tell, I had feared the reviews might this time have done me a very real injury with the buying public."[13]

Although William Michael Rossetti was wont to portray his sister as an instinctive and not particularly committed artist,[14] he occasionally implied the contrary. Discussing the composition of the poem "The Prince's Progress," he mentions a suggestion made by Dante Gabriel Rossetti. Christina, he tells us, "adopted the suggestion," but this was "almost the only instance in which she wrote anything so as to meet directly the views of another person." And in response to the self-posed question "Did Christina Rossetti consider herself truly a poetess and a good one?" he answered, "Truly a poetess, most decidedly yes; and, within the range of

11. Eugene J. Brzenk, "'Up-Hill' and 'Down-' by Christina Rossetti," *Victorian Poetry,* X (1972), 371.

12. Osbert Burdett, *The Beardsley Period: An Essay in Perspective* (New York, 1925), 131.

13. Packer (ed.), *The Rossetti-Macmillan Letters,* 89, 102, 105.

14. William Michael Rossetti (ed.), *Poetical Works of Christina Georgina Rossetti,* "Memoir," lxviii, lvi.

her subject and thought, and the limits of her executive endeavour, a good one. This . . . did render her very resolute in setting a line of demarcation between a person who is a poet and another person who is a versifier. . . . and she never could see any good reason why one who is not a poet should write in metre."[15]

Christina Rossetti's consciousness of the marketability of her name and her works is evident in a letter she wrote to "one of the many correspondents who pestered . . . [her] with endless requests for money in the 1880's." Instead of money, she sent him an autographed copy of her 1847 *Verses Dedicated to Her Mother,* which had been published privately by her grandfather, Gaetano Polidori. In the letter she wrote, "Perhaps you know that the common looking booklet before you fetches a fancy price now and then. . . . I have tried to make this copy a trifle more attractive by writing my name across the cover."[16] The shrewd, disciplined, and self-conscious artist suggested by these and similar statements is only beginning to be recognized.[17] Certainly, R. W. Crump's meticulous inclusion of the many variant readings of the poems will help to convince Rossetti readers of the care and thought that Rossetti put into the production and publication of the poems.

One of the most important poetic expressions of Rossetti's decision to dedicate herself to art is the 1849 poem "An End." Implicit in this seemingly simple little song is the speaker's rejection of realized love and her consequent commitment to art and the fantasies embodied in that art. The opening situation of "An End" will become a common one in Rossetti's poems: "Love, strong as Death, is dead." The demise of the vaguely personified Love moves her to sing graveside laments: "Sit we by his grave and sing / He is gone away." Although the speaker mourns the death of Love, she also suggests that the loss is not entirely regrettable; if Love was as "strong as Death" (a familiar notion to us by now), his removal from the speaker's world may be a blessing. Not only was Love a potentially destructive force, he was also fleeting and unreliable. Like the "dying flowers" on his bier, he partook of that natural transience that torments

15.   *Ibid.,* "Notes," 461, and "Memoir," lxix.

16.   Mark Samuels Lasner, "Christina Rossetti's 'Common Looking Booklet': A New Letter about her *Verses* of 1847," *Notes and Queries,* CCXXVI (1981), 420.

17.   See Antony H. Harrison, "Christina Rossetti: The Poetic Vocation," *Texas Studies in Literature and Language,* XXVII (1985), 225–46.

the speakers in other poems. Perhaps, then, the speaker's sorrow at the
passing of Love is only apparent; perhaps this death has been a good
thing. If Love is dead, she can escape his demands—the kind of demands
made upon the fair maiden in "Moonshine." Love's death exempts her
from dangerous involvement and allows her to create songs, or poetry:
"Sit we by his grave, and sing / He is gone away." Excused from a destructive relationship with Love, the speaker retreats into the world of art, to a
life of song-making. The subject of her art will be a form of fantasy, of
unreality.

> To few chords and sad and low
> Sing we so:
> Be our eyes fixed on the grass
> Shadow-veiled as the years pass,
> While we think of all that was
> In the long ago.
>
> (C, I: 38)

She will sing about love, but about *remembered* love, love that has been
reformed by the reshaping force of memory.

An untitled lyric included in Christina Rossetti's *Time Flies: A Reading
Diary* (1890), contains a complementary treatment of the relationship
between realized love and art. The poem ("My first roundel," wrote the
poet)[18] depicts a conflict between personifications of love and hope over
the advisability of romantic involvement. Love is cautious, timid, and
tedious (like Lizzie in "Goblin Market"); Hope is adventuresome and
imaginative (like Laura). Because Love refuses to engage precipitately in
romantic involvement, Hope must satisfy its longing with fantasies:

> Hope in dreams set off a-straying,
> All his dreamworld flushed by May;
> While unslumbering, praying, weighing
> Love said nay.[19]

Love represents, not the deathlike love of "Moonshine" and "An End,"
but the speaker's own suspicions about love. It watches and weighs and
hesitates because it is afraid. That such an attitude should be referred to as
"Love" is a good indication of the speaker's confused attitude toward that

18.   Quoted in Packer, *Christina Rossetti,* 432n11.
19.   Christina Rossetti, *Time Flies: A Reading Diary* (London, 1890), 86.

passion. For her, love is the warding off of passion and desire, not their reciprocation. Hope, on the other hand, signifies the ability of the imagination to create beautiful, unintimidating worlds. Hope represents, in short, the poet's own solution to the threats and inadequacies of reality— her assumption of the poetic career.

In 1848, Christina Rossetti began what was to become the tripartite poem "Three Stages," a work that indisputably reveals her strong commitment to the writing of poetry. Like much of Rossetti's very early work, the first poem of the series, "A Pause of Thought," is ambiguous in its references; its central subject is difficult to identify. The speaker has apparently spent much time pursuing an elusive but unidentified hope:

> I looked for that which is not, nor can be,
>   And hope deferred made my heart sick in truth:
>   But years must pass before a hope of youth
>   Is resigned utterly.
>
> (C, I: 51)

Although aware of the futility of her chase, she persists:

> Sometimes I said: It is an empty name
>   I long for; to a name why should I give
>   The peace of all the days I have to live?—
>   Yet gave it all the same.
>
> Alas, thou foolish one! alike unfit
>   For healthy joy and salutary pain:
>   Thou knowest the chase useless, and again
>   Turnest to follow it.
>
> (C, I: 52)

On the basis of the poem alone, there is no way to identify the speaker's aim; she could be referring to almost anything. Those biographers and critics who have studied the poem have concluded that its subject is love. In 1930, Edith Birkhead maintained that "'A Pause of Thought' . . . shows her [Rossetti's] hesitation and reluctance to abandon love." And according to Lona Mosk Packer, Christina Rossetti "had described the fruitless pursuit of love," revealing her "dilemma" about love "with . . . direct frankness"; this poem and the two that were later published with it, she continues, "deal with the theme of love."[20]

20.   Edith Birkhead, *Christina Rossetti and Her Poetry* (London, 1930), 50; Packer, *Christina Rossetti,* 82, 28–29.

Given the many other poems Rossetti wrote on the same subject during this period, Birkhead's and Packer's conclusions are plausible. In fact, the restless, dissatisfied speaker anticipates the speakers of some of the later love poems. But knowledge of the textual history of the poem broadens the interpretive possibilities. Although Christina Rossetti published this poem in the *Germ* in 1850 under the title "Thoughts Towards Nature in Poetry, Literature, and Art," the title of the original manuscript version was "Lines in Memory of Schiller's 'Der Pilgrim.'" (The title was not changed to "A Pause of Thought" until its appearance in the 1862 volume *Goblin Market and Other Poems*.)[21] It is reasonable to assume that a poem admittedly inspired by another work might treat the same subject. Schiller's concern in "Der Pilgrim" is not nearly as opaque as is Rossetti's in "A Pause of Thought." The speaker of his poem is also engaged in an ultimately futile quest:

> Abend ward's und wurde Morgen,
>   Nimmer, nimmer stand ich still,
> Aber immer blieb's verborgen,
>   Was ich suche, was ich will.[22]

In a similar manner, Rossetti's speaker

> watched and waited with a steadfast will:
>   And though the object seemed to flee away
> That I so longed for, ever day by day
>   I watched and waited still.
>
>   (C, I: 51–52)

In the Schiller poem, the goal of the speaker's search is identified: it is "dem Aufgang fort," a high career, which involves immortalizing transitory essences:

21.   R. W. Crump (ed.), *The Complete Poems of Christina Rossetti: A Variorum Edition* (Baton Rouge, 1979), I, 249–50.

22.   Eduard von der Hellen (ed.), *Schillers Samtliche Werke* (Stuttgart, 1904), I, 39. (All transcriptions of "Der Pilgrim" in this discussion derive from this text.)

The Poems of Schiller, trans. E. P. Arnold-Foster (London, 1903), 109, gives the following translation:

> Morn and eve in due procession
> Followed; never did I rest;
> But I sought in dark depression,
> Never nearer to my quest.

> Denn mich trieb ein mächtig Hoffen
> Und ein dunkles Glaubenswort;
> Wandle, rief's, der Weg ist offen,
> Immer nach dem Aufgang fort.
> Bis zu einer goldnen Pforten
> Du gelangst, da gehst du ein,
> Denn das Irdische wird dorten
> Himmlisch unvergänglich sein.[23]

The vocation that renders temporary, earthly objects immortal is that of the artist. The world beyond the golden portal where "das Irdische wird . . . Himmlisch unvergänglich" is similar to the world of Keats's artifact, the Grecian urn, where love is "forever panting, and forever young." Schiller's "Der Pilgrim" is a poem about art or, more specifically, about the difficulty of achieving artistic excellence. The similarities between the Schiller poem and Rossetti's "A Pause of Thought" strongly suggest that the goal of both searches is identical; if Schiller's aim is artistic excellence, then so too is Rossetti's. In "A Pause of Thought," the "empty name I long for" is the name of poet; the object of the "chase" (Schiller's "Was ich suche"), "the hope of youth," is poetic excellence or success.

Any remaining uncertainty about the identity of the subject of "A Pause of Thought" is convincingly dispelled by an examination of "The End of the First Part" (1849), the second in the series. This poem and a third written in 1854 were never published in the poet's lifetime, but they were linked in manuscript. William Michael Rossetti first published the poems as a unit under the title "Three Stages" in the 1896 volume of *New Poems*. In his notes to the 1904 edition of the *Poetical Works,* he attributes

---

23.   The Arnold-Foster translation:

> For a mighty inspiration
> Urged me on in tones sincere:—
> Saying "go, 'tis thy vocation
> To pursue a high career.
> If thou seest a golden portal
> Enter it without delay:
> Things of earth are there immortal
> And shall never pass away."

his sister's reticence to "their intimately personal character."[24] His sister's fastidiousness seems to have been unnecessary, for the second poem, like the first in the triad, obscures the identity of its subject in vagueness and abstractions. All the reader can discern is that the speaker, apparently unstimulated by her life, has found much joy in some form of fantasy, but that for mysterious reasons she has been ejected from the fantasy realm.

> Oh weary wakening from a life-true dream!
>   Oh pleasant dream from which I wake in pain!
> I rested all my trust on things that seem,
>   And all my trust is vain.
>
> (R: 288)

Exiled from her once-happy dreamworld, she resolves to live the remainder of her life in ascetic anticipation of death.

> But, where my palace stood, with the same stone
>   I will uprear a shady hermitage:
> And there my spirit shall keep house alone,
>   Accomplishing its age.
>
> (R: 289)

The precise nature of her "dream in which alone I lived so long" is never revealed, nor are the reasons for her departure from it. But, as in "A Pause of Thought," this difficulty is eased by knowledge of the work that influenced it.

Rossetti's poem was clearly composed under the strong influence of Tennyson's "The Palace of Art." That Christina Rossetti knew "The Palace of Art" well is confirmed by the strong resemblances between another of her poems, "From House to Home" (November 19, 1858), and the Tennyson work.[25] The two poems are strikingly similar in meter, language, imagery, theme, and movement. Tennyson's "Lordly pleasurehouse,"[26] his many-chambered palace of art, which signifies the life of the imagination, is echoed by the "palace" and "pleasure gardens" of

---

24. William Michael Rossetti (ed.), *Poetical Works of Christina Georgina Rossetti,* "Notes," 477.

25. See Stevenson, *The Pre-Raphaelite Poets,* 103.

26. The text of "The Palace of Art" is from Robert W. Hill, Jr. (ed.), *Tennyson's Poetry* (New York, 1971), 27–34.

Rossetti's poem. In both poems, the speakers' delight in their fantasy worlds ultimately deteriorates to a sense of sin and guilt. In "The Palace of Art," this guilt derives from the soul's great pride in its invulnerable isolation and power; in the Rossetti poem, it is not so easy to identify the speaker's sin. We are merely told,

> Now all the cherished secrets of my heart,
>   Now all my hidden hopes, are turned to sin.
> Part of my life is dead, part sick, and part
>   Is all on fire within.
>
> (R: 288)

(With this last line, compare Tennyson's "I am on fire within.") As penance for her crime, the soul of "The Palace of Art" plans to retreat to a sheltered retirement: "'Make me a cottage in the vale,' she said, / 'Where I may mourn and pray.'" In a similar spirit of contrition, Rossetti's persona will "uprear a shady hermitage" where "I will sit, and listen for the sound / Of the last lingering chime." While the Tennyson speaker leaves herself the option of returning to her palace "When I have purged my guilt," Rossetti's speaker sees no such possibility. In the final poem of the triad, she does, however, return to her "happy happy dream."

The imagery in the second and third poems of "Three Stages" helps to clarify both the speaker's perception of artistic creation and the extent of her commitment to her vocation. In "The End of the First Part," the central image is the garden. The happy, hopeful dream—the act of composing poetry—is referred to as "pleasure-gardens," and the speaker's ejection from the dream realm is represented as a vegetative deterioration:

> The fruitless thought of what I might have been,
>   Haunting me ever, will not let me rest.
> A cold North wind has withered all my green,
>   My sun is in the West.
>
> (R: 288)

She will retire to a hermitage equipped with another variety of garden: "There other garden-beds shall lie around, / Full of Sweet-briar and incense-bearing thyme." The poet's choice of garden imagery implies that the "happy dream" of careless, solitary artistic creation is for her a blissful paradisiacal state; but as in Eden, the perfection of creativity is destroyed by sin, presumably the sin of the poet's pride and self-isolation.

The final poem of "Three Stages" (untitled in manuscript but named "Restive" by William Michael Rossetti) details the speaker's gradual return to artistic creativity. This return is depicted as a reentry into a state of natural beauty and perfection:

> I felt the sunshine glow again, and knew
>   The swallow in its track:
> All birds awoke to building in the leaves,
> All buds awoke to fullness and sweet scent:
> Ah too my heart woke unawares, intent
>   On fruitful harvest sheaves.

(R: 290)

The speaker has recovered her paradise, but the composition of this garden and the speaker's attitude toward her retrieved creative bliss have altered significantly. Both are more humble and realistic: there are no more magnificent palaces, but merely the beauty of untouched nature. Further, the speaker's ecstasy is alloyed by the recognition of the impermanence of creative joy: "these joys may drift, as time now drifts along; / And cease, as once they ceased." Although her "heart" has reawakened, the speaker can no longer find the solace she once derived from her art. She realizes that the creative act is subject to the same transience and inadequacy that mar ordinary human life:

> I may pursue, and yet may not attain,
> Athirst and panting all the days I live:
> Or seem to hold, yet nerve myself to give
>   What once I gave, again.

(R: 290)

Her return to the artistic role may give her temporary satisfaction, but the speaker is aware in this final poem of the series that her fantasy world is no longer the perfect solution it had once been.

Throughout much of the early poetry, Rossetti makes this telling equation between her art and her vision of paradise—telling, because it is a further measure of the strength of her attachment to her vocation. This identification sheds interesting light on the many poems dealing with the subject of Paradise lost—poems, like "Shut Out" (1856), in which the speaker is again barred from reentering her edenic garden:

> The door was shut. I looked between
> > Its iron bars; and saw it lie,
> > My garden, mine, beneath the sky,
> Pied with all flowers bedewed and green.
>
> (C, I: 56)

As in the third poem of "Three Stages," she ultimately gains a much less satisfactory Paradise, one incapable of offering her the perfect beauty of the original:

> So now I sit here quite alone
> > Blinded with tears; nor grieve for that,
> > For nought is left worth looking at
> Since my delightful land is gone.
>
> A violet bed is budding near,
> > Wherein a lark has made her nest:
> > And good they are, but not the best;
> And dear they are, but not so dear.
>
> (C, I: 57)

The final two stanzas of this poem echo the ending of "The Lowest Room," though at a quick glance the poems may seem to have little in common. At the end of "The Lowest Room," the speaker, who among other things had longed for a creative gift like Homer's, ends up settling for a life as secluded and humble as the one depicted here. The simple, natural world of the final stanza of "Shut Out," with its budding flowers and nesting lark, is as pale an imitation of the speaker's fantasy world as was the simple domestic life chosen by the sister of the speaker in "The Lowest Room." But while the woman in "The Lowest Room" never had a chance to exercise poetic gifts or to take part in the glorious golden world of Homer, this speaker at one time did enjoy a paradisiacal experience of creativity. Her final exile from that world is not a welcome one, like the escape from the transforming experience of love in "Repining," but pained and regretful. The suggestion certainly is that while recovery from the failure of love is sometimes possible, recovery from the failure of creativity is very difficult.

Rossetti's representation of creative activity as an earthly paradise offering to its inhabitants intense joy and beauty, as a setting in which the inadequacies of life can be reshaped into new and entirely gratifying experiences, suggests that the artistic experience is virtually perfect. As poems like "Shut Out" indicate, the only disadvantage to the state of artistic creativity is that it, like the world it seeks to transform, is transient; one cannot sustain its intense pitch indefinitely. But as Rossetti continued to examine the creative act and to live the role of poet, she became disturbed by other flaws in this solution. Her growing ambivalence about the function of art informs the well-known sonnet "In An Artist's Studio" (1856), among her most important expressions of the risks inherent in creative activity.

Graceful and seemingly simple, this sonnet is a rich and acute representation of Rossetti's understanding of the complicated, and potentially dangerous, relationship between art and life. In the poem, Christina and a companion, while touring Dante Gabriel Rossetti's studio, come upon picture after picture of Lizzie Siddal, the woman Dante Gabriel was to marry in 1860.

> One face looks out from all his canvases,
>   One selfsame figure sits or walks or leans:
>   We found her hidden just behind those screens,
>   That mirror gave back all her loveliness.
> A queen in opal or in ruby dress,
>   A nameless girl in freshest summer-greens,
>   A saint, an angel—every canvas means
>   The same one meaning, neither more nor less.
>
>   (R: 330)

The octave sets up the central theme of the poem: the contradiction between art and the reality it works from but ultimately transforms. Here the contradiction is primarily between the many and the one—between the multiple, painted versions of Lizzie and "the same one meaning" behind those versions. The *single* interpretation is emphasized by the repetition of the word "one" in the octave—"one face," "one selfsame figure," "same one meaning." Even the repeated subject-verb syntactical pattern of the opening four-line sentence ("face looks," "figure sits," "we found," "mirror gave") underlines the monotony of the paintings' meaning. Set against this singleness are many expressions of plurality, of alternatives: "all his canvases," "sits or walks or leans," "screens," "A queen . . . A nameless girl . . . A saint, an angel." Despite the poet's insistence on the single meaning of all these possibilities, we do not at this point know what that one meaning is.

It is not until the sestet, which introduces the relationship between Dante Gabriel, the woman he paints, and the paintings themselves, that the "same one meaning" is quietly revealed.

> He feeds upon her face by day and night,
>   And she with true kind eyes looks back on him,
> Fair as the moon and joyful as the light:
>   Not wan with waiting, not with sorrow dim;
> Not as she is, but was when hope shone bright;
>   Not as she is, but as she fills his dream.

> (R: 330)

For Dante Gabriel, the gift for turning reality (Lizzie) into art (the paintings) has been positive: it has allowed him to transform the unsatisfactory Lizzie, "wan with waiting . . . with sorrow dim," into a beautiful woman, "Fair as the moon and joyful as the light"—indeed, into many beautiful women. It is clear to the poet that these fantasized versions of Lizzie give their painter far more pleasure than he can derive from the woman herself. For Dante Gabriel, as well as for Christina, it is "better to dream than wake, for oh in waking / The sights are not so fair."

But as the language of the poem demonstrates, it is equally clear to Christina that Lizzie has been deprived, diminished, and entrapped. While his work creates for the artist multiple possibilities, it does so, not by revealing his subject's mutable and complex reality, but by reducing and denying it. The face that "looks out" in line 1 suggests a kind of imprisonment, as does the past participle "hidden" in line 3; in line 4, "gave back" suggests primarily "reflects," but also the restitution of something that has been taken away. And in what is the most powerful line of the poem, "He feeds upon her face by day and night" (line 9), the emphasis is on Dante Gabriel's destructive appetite—an appetite that does not diminish the picture itself, which steadily remains the same ("And she with true kind eyes looks back on him"), but that must have diminished the real Lizzie.

Lizzie, as the painter's subject, is in the same danger as the women in Rossetti's poems who enter into illusory romantic relationships only to find themselves entrapped and reduced. Lizzie's plight is doubly dangerous because she is in fact involved in just such a relationship with Dante Gabriel, *and* she is being somehow reduced by his efforts to transform her through his art. Although Christina never makes explicit a causality between her brother's preoccupation with painting Lizzie and the real Lizzie's unhappy condition, the poem strongly suggests that Lizzie has grown wan and sorrowful—has literally wasted away—through Dante Gabriel's attempts to turn her into something she is not. The actual relationship between Dante Gabriel Rossetti and Lizzie Siddall seems to have been exactly the way Christina portrayed it in this poem. It was unquestionably Lizzie's beauty that first attracted Dante Gabriel, and he was obsessed with painting that beauty in all sorts of settings, even as Lizzie herself became a "broken and embittered invalid," waiting for ten years for Dante Gabriel to marry her.[27]

In the sonnet, Christina sees that the loser is not the artist but the person (the experience, the reality) that the artist seeks to transform. This finally is "the same one meaning" of all the paintings of Lizzie—that the artist can so prefer the artifact that he will never willingly return to the comparatively pallid original. Or reduced to its simplest level, the "one meaning" of the many beautiful paintings of Lizzie is the sad truth that Dante Gabriel loves not the real woman but the false women that he has created in his work. Rossetti's insistence on the single interpretation of the many paintings seems to recall the point made in "Amor Mundi" about the dangers of multifaceted signs. But it is important to recognize that in "In An Artist's Studio," the "same one meaning" is not an all-encompassing truth that makes sense out of confusion (as in "Goblin Market"), but a lie that inverts the enriching powers of art. Dante Gabriel's paintings of Lizzie do not *reveal* truth, as his sister's poetry will come to do, but *falsify* it. The admonishments contained in this important sonnet had a powerful effect on the aesthetic position that Christina Rossetti was in the process of developing.

Writing poetry offered Christina Rossetti a method for intensifying and preserving experience, for eluding the conventional female roles, and for recasting reality altogether. Despite their risks, these transformative functions of art were enormously compelling for Rossetti; they were what

27. Oswald Doughty, *A Victorian Romantic: Dante Gabriel Rossetti* (London, 1949), 262.

drew her to the poetic vocation. Much of Rossetti's most important and well-known poetry is driven by this transforming, reformulating imperative. In many poems, she hides behind the creations of her imagination and substitutes them for a painful reality. But in these works, she eludes the dangers raised in "In An Artist's Studio"; she does not exhaust the possibilities of a vital reality by rejecting it in favor of artistic fantasies, but rather reshapes the barren landscape of her personal losses into vibrant and tolerable forms. In the later work, including most of her religious poems, she uses the poetic process as a way of finding the truth, not hiding from it. Finally, for Rossetti, the miracle of poetic creation is its potential for discovery, its ability to reveal the powerfully reforming truth. Rossetti was conscious of the potential dangers of the poetic vocation, but she grew to believe that they could be avoided as long as poetry was written to discover the truth. This view, which came out of her personal need to reformulate experience and which blended well with the principles of her religious faith, became the foundation of her personal aesthetic.

THREE

Reparative Strategies

ince the time of Christina Rossetti's death, her compelling and mysterious love poems have attracted the interest of critics, biographers, and casual readers of the poetry. Although these poems constitute roughly one quarter of the extant poetry, they have received much more critical attention than has any other group of poems, including the religious poetry, which makes up at least half of the total canon. The artistic excellence of many of the love poems may partially account for their centrality in Rossetti criticism; this group contains some of Rossetti's most accomplished work. But as powerful as the appeal of their artistry is, even more intriguing are the mysterious circumstances that inspired such remarkable verse. Like Shakespeare's sonnets or Arnold's Marguerite poems, Rossetti's impassioned love poetry creates curiosity about its biographical source. Unfortunately, in some all-too-influential cases, this curiosity to identify individuals has eclipsed the equally important need to study the poems themselves—not simply as biographical documents, but as important works of art reflecting an intricate complex of personal experience, acute observation, and social and cultural influences. To assume that Christina Rossetti's love poetry can be reduced to a simple and single biographical correlative is a sadly reductive approach to a poet whose work, despite (or possibly because of) her own discomfort with ambiguity, is such a masterly expression of the conflicts and ambiguities of the human condition.

That these poems are important, there can be no doubt. They demonstrate the wide range of Rossetti's artistic skill and the depth to which her imagination was penetrated by what must have seemed to her the single verity of love: it does not last. For it is not *love* that Christina Rossetti wrote about again and again, but the failure of love. The secular poetry of the 1840s, 1850s, and 1860s is repeatedly based on the assumption, or reaches the conclusion, that romantic love inevitably ends in some form of betrayal and heartbreaking loss.

Throughout this period, the renderings of failed love are varied and experimental. Among this group are sonnets, ballads, long poems, short poems, dialogues, trilogues, monologues; female speakers, male speakers, speakers whose sex is indeterminate; densely imagistic poems, and easy, conversational poems. The variations on the central theme are as numerous: in the most common scenario, a man betrays a loving woman, usually through inconstancy, but sometimes through indifference; occasionally, the woman abandons the man (in these cases, because of an unspecified guilt over the relationship or because of her indifference toward him); sometimes the relationship is ended by the death of the man, sometimes by the death of the woman; and in a few particularly interesting poems, the woman is dragged away from a seemingly happy relationship by the ghost of a former lover. That as few as a half dozen poems in the Rossetti canon present an immediate and happy relationship (for example, "A Birthday," "Maiden-Song," "The Lowest Room," and "A Bride Song") only confirms the inveteracy of Rossetti's conviction about romantic love.

Although related, the love poems discussed in Chapter Two and the poems about failed love to be examined here differ in significant ways. In those considered earlier, a fully realized relationship is seen as dangerous to the woman; in the others, such a relationship is presented as impossible—usually, but not always, because of some betrayal on the man's part. In these poems, love threatens through its instability, not through its permanence. Poems such as "Moonshine" represent the speaker's unsuccessful attempt to *transform* a dissatisfying life through the magic of romantic love; but the poems about failed love (a much larger group) portray romantic love, with its inevitable disappointments and desertions, as itself in need of transformation. Taken together, these two groups of poems reflect an utterly hopeless view of love between men and women: according to these poems, realized romantic relationships, vulnerable to permanence and transience, commitment and inconstancy, fate and volition, have no hope of survival.

Without question, Rossetti's insistently bleak representations of love reflect profoundly influential experiences, observations, and pressures in her own life. Christina Rossetti was no stranger to the disappointments of love: her two broken engagements, the lingering illness and death of her father, the separations of many in her own circle must have discouraged her. When to these personal experiences and observations we add the influence of her adolescent reading of Keats, Scott, Maturin, and Radcliffe, all of whom wrote in the literary tradition of failed love, we recognize how inevitable love's failure must have seemed to her. Rossetti's life coincided with the century's literary obsession with the theme of failed love, reflected in the works of Dante Gabriel Rossetti, Keats, Scott, Arnold, Tennyson, Swinburne, Meredith, and Hardy, and in the poems of less recognized writers like Fanny Kemble, Caroline Norton, Letitia Landon, and Caroline Lamb. Though Rossetti's interest in failed love was by no means unique among her contemporaries, she reworked the theme more persistently than most did.[1]

Rossetti's "pitiless examination of the root patterns of betrayal" may not be "*the* great value [my emphasis]" of her work, but it is certainly *a* great value requiring more attention than it has received.[2] In the last few years, a number of promising articles on individual poems or small groups of poems within the larger group of failed-love poems have appeared— articles eschewing the exclusively biographical approach in favor of closer analyses of the poems themselves.[3] But a broader examination of the general patterns of the entire group is also needed. To date, Lona Mosk Packer's biography of Christina Rossetti contains the only detailed investigation of this group of poems as a whole, but that investigation is seriously flawed by its preoccupation with *identifying* the male lover. This chapter examines the poems about failed love with the objective of establishing the critical connection between the poet's conviction about relationships and her own art. While the inevitability of love's failure constituted a tremendous loss to Christina Rossetti, from it came a greater gain: the urge to repair, to transform, to create, and, in the best of circumstances, to discover new truths. As these poems repeatedly prove, loss was the well-

1. Kathleen Hickok, *Representations of Women: Nineteenth-Century British Women's Poetry* (Westport, Conn., 1984), 20–32.

2. McGann, "Christina Rossetti's Poems: A New Edition and a Revaluation," 241.

3. See, for example, Rees, "Christina Rossetti: Poet"; and Michie, "The Battle for Sisterhood."

spring of creativity for Rossetti, and creativity a method of discovery.

For a young girl brought up in a time that endorsed only one accept-able adult female role—that of being loved and protected by a man—the realization that this very relationship was for her impossible must have been hugely disruptive. In her poetry, Rossetti found a way to repair the breach in her life caused by her unbearable discovery about love and a means through which deprivation could be turned into creativity. Her love poetry was almost never used as an instrument for the masochistic probing of wounds, as some have suggested; rather, it was a way of distancing herself from severe pain, of escaping it by reshaping its cause, and of discovering important truths through this impulse to transform. Indeed, though her poetry abounds with broken relationships, only a few poems concentrate on the pain and disappointment that follow the rup-ture. Most of the poems in the failed-love group are an attempt to escape the pain, not to relive it.

Unquestionably, Rossetti recognized and made use of the distancing and reshaping properties of art; she was aware that writing poetry about the painful conditions of her life *changed* those conditions, gave them a quality comfortably distinct from their real essence. Pain—disordered, shapeless, intolerable—is not preserved in a poem as much as it is changed, ordered, reduced into a manageable shape. The act of turning her experiences into poetry enabled Rossetti to achieve desperately needed distance from her difficult discoveries about the role of love in her life. But, as we shall see, she needed more distance from this truth than she could gain from poetically representing it. So, in most of the poems in this group, she introduces strategies by which the experience, already re-formed by being turned into art, can be reshaped and distanced still further. Through the transforming properties inherent in memory, fan-tasy, anticipation, and fiction, Rossetti creates something new and positive out of love's failure. The most intricate of these poems are like nests of Chinese boxes, with recesses within recesses—re-formed reality within re-formed reality. There are subtle variants to fantasy, memory, anticipa-tion, and fiction, and each functions uniquely, but the result is the same: the recasting of an initial, unhappy situation into a tolerable and, in many cases, joyful one.

From the time she began writing poetry, Christina Rossetti was preoccupied with the problem of love's failure. Most of the dramatic variations and the transforming strategies used in the later, failed-love poems first appeared in the verse Rossetti wrote before the age of seventeen (labeled "Juvenilia" by William Michael Rossetti in the 1904 *Poetical Works*). By the age of eighteen, when she wrote "An End," Rossetti had a clear under-standing of the part that love would play in her life and in her poetry. Given the direction her poetry would take, "An End" reads like a self-conscious poetic manifesto. In this poem, Rossetti announces that while love will not be a part of her life, it will be a major part of her poetry. As do most of the poems from the failed-love group, "An End" begins with love's failure: "Love, strong as Death, is dead." Here, as in the related poems, none of the particulars about Love are provided—whether he is a real person or an abstract personification of all romantic relationships, or why he has disappeared. The speaker only suggests rather cryptically in the second stanza that Love left because he could not withstand the passage of time:

> He was born in the Spring,
> And died before the harvesting:
> On the last warm Summer day
> He left us; he would not stay
> For Autumn twilight cold and gray.
> (C, I: 38)

As is usually the case in these poems, the speaker concentrates, not on the details of Love's dissolution, but on how she will manage his disap-pearance from her life. In this poem, she identifies two curative methods: poetry and memory. First, the speaker eases her pain over Love's passing by *singing* (writing poetry) about his departure.

> Sit we by his grave, and sing
> He is gone away.
>
> To few chords and sad and low
> Sing we so.
> (C, I: 38)

These lines serve as a near-perfect proleptic characterization of the love poems Rossetti will write for the next twenty years: they are songs about the many ways in which men and women are failed by love. The speaker mitigates her suffering still further by remembering:

Be our eyes fixed on the grass
Shadow-veiled as the years pass,
While we think of all that was
In the long ago.

(C, I: 38)

By concentrating on the presumably happy memory "of all that was / In the long ago," the speaker distances herself still further from an unhappy and transient love. For memory shares the transforming properties of art: like art, it too selectively reshapes experience and renders timeless what is otherwise subject to change and corruption. Singing songs about remembered love puts the speaker at two removes from the initial situation and allows her to transform a love that was transient and painful into one that is permanent and comforting. In her dedication to the artistic memorialization of Love, then, the speaker (and, clearly, Rossetti herself) finds a precious refuge from much that pained her about her own experience.

The double poem "Memory" (the first part written in 1857, the second in 1865) expands the position first developed in "An End." Part I of "Memory" (originally entitled "A Blank") consists of a more detailed, but still cryptic, exposition of the death of Love. Here, the decision to terminate a relationship is made by the speaker herself.

I nursed it in my bosom while it lived,
    I hid it in my heart when it was dead;
In joy I sat alone, even so I grieved
        Alone and nothing said.

I shut the door to face the naked truth,
    I stood alone—I faced the truth alone,
Stripped bare of self-regard or forms or ruth
        Till first and last were shown.

I took the perfect balances and weighed;
    No shaking of my hand disturbed the poise;
Weighed, found it wanting: not a word I said,
        But silent made my choice.

None know the choice I made; I make it still.
    None know the choice I made and broke my heart,
Breaking mine idol: I have braced my will
        Once, chosen for once my part.

I broke it at a blow, I laid it cold,
  Crushed in my deep heart where it used to live.
My heart dies inch by inch; the time grows old,
  Grows old in which I grieve.

(C, I: 147–48)

As in "An End," the references to this love are so abstract and impersonal that it is difficult to believe she is talking about a real relationship. In "Memory," the speaker never refers to a *person* at all, but uses the pronoun "it" throughout. The poem might be about her attitude toward the role of love in general, not one particular man, in her life. Certainly this would help to explain the curious suggestion (l. 3) that even when this love was most fulfilling, the speaker was solitary: "In joy I sat alone." Or the impersonal reference could be a way to ward off the intense pain revived through remembering her decision. Certainly the immediate effect of this decision ("My heart dies inch by inch") has been horrible, leaving the speaker aged, alone, and, worst of all, incapable of reformulating the situation in any positive way. At this point, she can only use her poetry to "sing / He is gone away," as did the speaker of "An End." Her inability to look beyond the event, or even behind it to the earlier joy, is reflected by the repetitive language of the poem. Throughout the five stanzas, the speaker repeats words, phrases, and syntactical patterns: "None know the choice I made; I make it still" (l. 13) is substantially repeated in "None know the choice I made and broke my heart" (l. 14); "I shut the door to face the naked truth" (l. 5) is echoed by "I stood alone—I faced the truth alone" (l. 6). It is as if the speaker can move forward in her discourse only with great difficulty—as if, unable to find a way out of rehearsing the pain, she can only retrace old ground.

In Part II (composed in 1865 under the title "A Memory"), the speaker remains preoccupied with the failed relationship, but the passage of time has provided her an escape from the deadening stasis of Part I. The rehearsal of her pain has given way to the expedient of memory, which has transformed the truth into a positive source of consolation.

I have a room whereinto no one enters
  Save I myself alone:
There sits a blessed memory on a throne,
  There my life centres;

While winter comes and goes—oh tedious comer!—
  And while its nip-wind blows;
  While bloom the bloodless lily and warm rose
Of lavish summer.

If any should force entrance he might see there
  One buried yet not dead,
  Before whose face I no more bow my head
Or bend my knee there;

But often in my worn life's autumn weather
  I watch there with clear eyes,
  And think how it will be in Paradise
When we're together.

(C, I: 148)

Time has softened the speaker's pain and given her a medium by which to reconstitute the shattered love of Part I into a happy whole. Quite literally, she has re-membered him, put him back together, but this time in different shape. This transformation is the perfect solution for the speaker, particularly because she does not seem to want to forget the lover entirely. The transformed version is entirely private—"I have a room whereinto no one enters / Save I myself alone"; it is permanent—"There my life centres; / While winter comes and goes"; and it is far less costly emotionally than is the relationship itself—"I no more bow my head / Or bend my knee there." The speaker's self-conscious, deliberate description of this transforming process demonstrates Rossetti's awareness of the enormous power of memory, which can turn reality into something it never was, something that serves the speaker far better than pain, certainly, but perhaps serves better than even the relationship itself. And unlike most memories, this one has a future as well as a past: the speaker's faith in Heaven allows her the luxury of contemplating an anticipated reunion with this remembered love.

That the expedient of memory is successful is documented by the difference in pace and tone between the two parts of this poem. In Part II, the hesitations and repetitions of Part I have entirely disappeared; the shorter second and fourth lines in each stanza and the many instances of enjambment in Part II create a quick-paced, confident, goal-directed discourse—one vastly different from the imaginative stasis of Part I.

The transforming properties of memory do not fail Rossetti often, but when they do, her regret is poignant. In the *Monna Innominata* sonnet sequence, Rossetti shows a woman's repeated and varied attempts to contend with the failure of an intense romantic relationship. The speaker looks to memory, in the second sonnet, to assuage the pain of separating from her lover, but memory is unusually delinquent.

> I wish I could remember that first day,
>> First hour, first moment of your meeting me,
>> If bright or dim the season, it might be
> Summer or Winter for aught I can say;
> So unrecorded did it slip away,
>> So blind was I to see and to foresee,
>> So dull to mark the budding of my tree
> That would not blossom yet for many a May.
> If only I could recollect it, such
>> A day of days! I let it come and go
>> As traceless as a thaw of bygone snow;
> It seemed to mean so little, meant so much;
> If only now I could recall that touch,
>> First touch of hand in hand—Did one but know!
>> (C, II: 87)

The speaker needs some raw material from which to fashion a consoling memory, and that material is not available. This is the only time in the sequence that she seeks comfort from memory; she goes on to examine other strategies for managing her pain but finds that most of them, with the possible exception of anticipation, are finally useless. In its entirety, the *Monna Innominata* group affirms romantic love as an abstract ideal but despairs about the likelihood of its survival in both a real and a fantastic (imagined, remembered) world.

The sonnet "Remember" (1849) is among Christina Rossetti's richest treatments of memory, though here its distancing, reshaping function is put to a rather different use. Consisting of a dying woman's farewell to her lover, the poem subtly represents the speaker's ambivalence about a prospectively permanent romantic relationship. The situation of the poem is this: A dying woman, apparently afraid of the impending oblivion of death, implores her lover, or fiancé ("You tell me of our future that you planned"), to remember her after her death. It is as if the speaker has taken the scenario of "An End," cast herself in the role of Love, and the man in the role of the lover who lives on to memorialize the relationship.

Remember me when I am gone away,
  Gone far away into the silent land;
  When you can no more hold me by the hand,
Nor I half turn to go yet turning stay.
Remember me when no more day by day
  You tell me of our future that you planned:
  Only remember me; you understand
It will be late to counsel then or pray.
Yet if you should forget me for a while
  And afterwards remember, do not grieve:
  For if the darkness and corruption leave
  A vestige of the thoughts that once I had,
Better by far you should forget and smile
  Than that you should remember and be sad.

(C, I: 37)

The foundation of the poem—the truth of the situation—is the speaker's feelings about the man she addresses. While he appears to love her, to be planning their future, she does not love him, or, at the least, she is discomfited by his assumptions. This truth is well hidden within ambiguous language and cryptic references, but it is accessible nonetheless. An attentive reading of the octave suggests that the couple's relationship has not been ideally romantic. The woman describes with decided ambiguity certain activities that her death will terminate: "When you can no more hold me by the hand, / Nor I half turn to go yet turning stay. / Remember me when no more day by day / You tell me of our future that you planned." These lines suggest an unacted-upon desire to leave the man ("I half turn to go yet turning stay") and a constrained passivity reminiscent of "Moonshine" ("you can no more hold me by the hand," "You tell me of our future that you planned"). While such passivity may have reflected contemporary expectations of female behavior, it is still difficult to imagine that a woman as actively creative and ultimately independent as Christina Rossetti could have willingly accepted this position. The implications of the octave are substantiated by the conclusion of the sonnet. The "thoughts that once I had," only a "vestige" of which, if remembered, would make the man sad, must have been unkind (but unspoken) thoughts about him and about the future that he planned. In short, the speaker does not want the man to know how she really feels about him. In light of her reticence about the man and their future, her death must be seen, not as a tragic end to the relationship, but as a welcome release. It is remarkable that telling the truth—declaring that she neither loves nor needs the man—should be so unthinkable. But for a woman of Rossetti's time, who learned, at a young age, the catechism of female dependence, such a declaration of independence would be apostasy, harder and more painful to imagine even than her own death.

Beneath the casual, conversational, deceptively simple language of the sonnet lies a dense rendering of the multiple functions of memory. The speaker's repeated request to be remembered must be read against the truth of her negative feelings about him; we can appreciate the evolving ambiguity of the five usages of "remember" only after her attitude is clarified. In the first two lines, the request appears to originate in her fear of oblivion ("Remember me when I am gone away, / Gone far away into the silent land"). But by the third occurrence of the words "remember me," in line 7, the request has acquired a different meaning. In view of the suggestions throughout the octave of the speaker's own ambivalence, the phrase becomes a desperate request for *separation,* not for lasting remembrance. By lines 7 and 8, when the speaker implores the man to "Only remember me; you understand / It will be late to counsel then or pray," we realize that she could not tolerate his apparently dominating treatment of her—that "only" being remembered, not counseled or besought, not held or planned for, would be a huge relief. The act of remembering distances the speaker from an undesirable situation; the difference is that here the woman will be the memory itself, not the rememberer. Here she escapes, not the pain of a failed relationship, but the discomfort of a dissatisfying alliance. Implicit throughout her injunction is her recognition that memory is useful only if it transforms and softens the truth; as she tells the man at the end of the sonnet, if remembering merely preserves pain and truth, "the thoughts that once I had" (as it did in Part I of "Memory"), "better by far . . . forget and smile / Than that you should remember and be sad."

As we saw in the second poem of the *Monna Innominata* sequence, memory, to operate effectively, must have some foundation in fact. But Rossetti was also capable of managing her disappointment about love by spinning fantasies fueled solely by her intense wish that things could be otherwise. Unlike the poems in which memory softens pain over time, the works in which Rossetti resorts to outright fantasy tend to be emotionally overwrought and give the impression of a desperate groping for a trans- forming anodyne. This desperation is apparent in "Heart's Chill Be- tween," one of the first poems about a perfidious lover and virtually *the* first failed-love poem to resort to wishing and pretending as reshaping strategies. It may have been the poem's desperate quality that made William Michael Rossetti omit it from the 1896 edition of his sister's poetry, *New Poems*. Written in 1847 under the title "The Last Hope," the poem appeared under its new name in the *Athenaeum* on October 14, 1848, and was the first poem by Christina Rossetti published in a major literary journal. The latter fact alone makes its exclusion from the 1896 edition surprising. But according to William Michael, "As it comes in point of date, near the close of the *Juvenilia,* it ought to have been better than it is, and was hardly good enough for re-publication." He did, however, choose to include it in the 1904 *Poetical Works* because "the revival of the poem by Mr. Bell [presumably in Bell's 1898 biography of Christina Rossetti] alters the conditions somewhat."[4]

The poem consists almost entirely of the speaker's description of the pain—immediate and unabating—caused by a lover's long-past betrayal. (Such a concentration upon the pain of separation is unusual in Rossetti's poems about failed love.) In the first two stanzas of the poem, the speaker describes her initial reaction to the discovery of her lover's inconstancy:

> I did not chide him, though I knew
>   That he was false to me.
> Chide the exhaling of the dew,
>   The ebbing of the sea,
> The fading of a rosy hue—
>   But not inconstancy.
>
> Why strive for love when love is o'er—
>   Why bind a restive heart?
> He never knew the pain I bore
>   In saying—"We must part,
> Let us be friends and nothing more":
>   Oh woman's shallow art!
>
>   (R: 109)

4.   William Michael Rossetti (ed.), *Poetical Works of Christina Georgina Rossetti,* "Notes," 467.

The depth of her despair about love is revealed in her suggestion that inconstancy is more predictable and ineluctable than "the exhaling of the dew, / The ebbing of the sea." Years later, the nonchalance she affected earlier has become real, or so she tries to convince the reader.

> But it is over, it is done:
>   I hardly heed it now:
> So many weary years have run
>   Since then I think not how
> Things might have been—but greet each one
>   With an unruffled brow.
>
> What time I am where others be
>   My heart seems very calm—
> Stone-calm.

(R: 109)

But her "calm," "unruffled" demeanor is really only a mask she has created (more of "woman's shallow art") to hide her continuing pain. Despite the passage of "many weary years," she remains deeply affected by her loss. The speaker's description of the mental anguish she tries to hide from friends is probably the most chilling and emotionally immediate of any of its kind in the Rossetti canon:

> but, if all go from me,
>   There comes a vague alarm,
> A shrinking in the memory
>   From some forgotten harm.
>
> And often through the long long night,
>   Waking when none are near,
> I feel my heart beat fast with fright,
>   Yet know not what I fear:
> Oh how I long to see the light,
>   And the sweet birds to hear!
>
> To have the sun upon my face,
>   To look up through the trees,
> To walk forth in the open space
>   And listen to the breeze,—
> And not to dream the burial-place
>   Is clogging my weak knees.
>
> Sometimes I can nor weep nor pray,

But am half stupefied;
And then all those who see me say
Mine eyes are opened wide
And that my wits seem gone astray:—
Ah would that I had died!

(R: 109)

The speaker tries to manage her enormous pain in a number of ways, one of which is simply expressing the pain, letting out the fears and feelings that overwhelm her (stanzas 4 and 5). She also tries to escape her true feelings by adopting a false pose, by pretending. To her lover (stanza 1) and to her friends (stanza 4), the speaker dissembles, creating a mask that disguises her real feelings.[5] But in solitude, the pain of her lover's earlier defection is so overwhelming that it defeats the strategy of the mask. At first, she can only helplessly describe her feelings, but in stanzas 5 and 6, she is briefly able to grab hold of one more strategy—that of wishing herself into another world. For six lines, she manages to create a refuge for herself through wishing and words, but her pain is so intense that this strategy finally breaks down as well.

Oh how I long to see the light,
And the sweet birds to hear!

To have the sun upon my face,
To look up through the trees,
To walk forth in the open space
And listen to the breeze,—
And not to dream the burial-place
Is clogging my weak knees.

(R: 109)

The breakdown of all these methods, rare in Rossetti's poetry, gives us a measure of the overpowering, incapacitating effects of the failed love affair. Without the lament or the mask or the wish, the speaker experiences a kind of catatonia:

Sometimes I can nor weep nor pray,
But am half stupefied;

5.   For an interesting discussion of Rossetti's use of the poetic voice as a mask, see Harrison, "Christina Rossetti: The Poetic Vocation."

> And then all those who see me say
> Mine eyes are opened wide
> And that my wits seem gone astray:—
> Ah would that I had died!
>
> (R: 109)

For Rossetti, this inability to express pain, to formulate a wish, or to re-form experience is the ultimate nightmare: the poet's Hell of muteness. (This condition appears in only a few of her poems. Two of the finest renderings of the poet's muteness are the 1855 sonnet "Cobwebs" and the fourteenth sonnet of the *Monna Innominata* sequence.) With her creative, transforming powers impotent, the speaker can only look to death for relief. As much as she fears death (she has nightmares of "the burial-place / . . . clogging my weak knees"), it is preferable to this incoherent stupefaction:

> Would I could die and be at peace—
> Or living could forget!
> My grief nor grows nor doth decrease,
> But ever is. And yet
> Methinks now that all this shall cease
> Before the sun shall set.
>
> (R: 109)

Here, as in many of the poems about lost love, death becomes a third strategy, "the last hope" (the poem's original title) when masks and words and fantasies are ineffectual.

One week after the composition of "Heart's Chill Between," Christina Rossetti wrote "Death's Chill Between," also omitted by William Michael from *New Poems*. The situations of the poems are similar, but in the later poem, the speaker has been bereaved, not betrayed. "Death's Chill Between," according to William Michael, "was originally named *Anne of Warwick,* and was intended to represent (in a rather 'young-ladyish' form) the dolorous emotions and flitting frenzy of Anne, when widowed of her youthful husband, the Prince of Wales, slain after the battle of Tewkesbury."[6]

6. William Michael Rossetti (ed.), *Poetical Works of Christina Georgina Rossetti,* "Notes," 467.

At the outset of the poem, the recently widowed speaker suffers the same mute pain as that experienced by the woman in "Heart's Chill Between":

> You can go,—I shall not weep;
>   You can go unto your rest.
> My heart-ache is all too deep,
>   And too sore my throbbing breast.
> Can sobs be, or angry tears,
> Where are neither hopes nor fears?
>
> (R: 110)

Before long, the speaker is able to transform this hopeless condition into joy through a fantasy far more extreme and extended than the wishful words of the earlier poem, which for six brief lines gave that speaker a respite from her suffering. In "Death's Chill Between," the speaker's fantasy-wish is also more successful: she is able to convince herself of its truth for most of the poem. Her belief in the transforming fantasy is what William Michael refers to, rather deprecatingly, as Anne's "flitting frenzy": it is a form of madness.

> Listen, listen!—Everywhere
>   A low voice is calling me,
> And a step is on the stair,
>   And one comes you do not see.
> Listen, listen!—Evermore
> A dim hand knocks at the door.
>
> Hear me! He is come again,
>   My own dearest is come back.
> Bring him in from the cold rain;
>   Bring wine, and let nothing lack.
> Thou and I will rest together,
> Love, until the sunny weather.
>
> (R: 111)

Only at the end of the poem does this mad-fantasy strategy fail the speaker:

> Who hath talked of weeping?—Yet
>   There is something at my heart
> Gnawing, I would fain forget,

And an aching and a smart.—
Ah, my mother, 'tis in vain,
For he is not come again.

(R: 111)

Despite this final failure, this poem, even more than its immediate predecessor, reveals Rossetti's early experimentation with the reshaping powers of the imagination. Here, her evocation of these powers is rather clumsy and simplistic, but before long, she will recognize and express their complexity with remarkable skill.

As Rossetti matured as a poet, she employed the transforming properties of fantasy more skillfully. The later love poems tend to be more emotionally restrained and use fantasy in a more sophisticated manner than do the early poems, but the theme (the failure of love) and the objective (transforming that failure through language and imagination) remain virtually the same. An excellent example of the coexistence of formal development with thematic continuity is the sonnet "Touching 'Never.'" The actual composition date of this poem is unknown; it first appeared in the 1881 volume *A Pageant and Other Poems,* and William Michael affixed a "Before 1882" date to it in the *Poetical Works.* Given its resemblance to other later poems, the verse was almost certainly written during Rossetti's maturity.

Faced with the apparently hopeless situation of loving someone who does not love her, the speaker of "Touching 'Never'" composes three arguments by which to convince the man that his indifference could change to love. Unable to accept his neutrality (unable, as the title suggests, to imagine the implications of "never"), the speaker resorts in the first quatrain to the rather empty and unoriginal proposition "Where there's life, there's hope."

Because you never yet have loved me, dear,
    Think you you never can nor ever will?
    Surely while life remains hope lingers still,
Hope the last blossom of life's dying year.

(C, II: 102)

In the second quatrain, the speaker comes up with a more complicated, and perhaps more persuasive, argument. Borrowing evidence from nature, she argues for the possibility of change and renewal:

> Because the season and mine age grow sere,
>   Shall never Spring bring forth her daffodil,
>   Shall never sweeter Summer feast her fill
> Of roses with the nightingales they hear?
>
> (C, II: 102)

After setting up the analogy between the current season (presumably autumn) and her own advancing age ("Because the season and mine age grow sere"), the speaker implies that she, like nature, might enjoy a renewal. First, by mentioning the promise of spring, she suggests her own potential for regeneration ("Shall never Spring bring forth her daffodil"); then, cleverly, she escalates her argument by suggesting how much better even than spring is summer. The promise of summer is presented as sensually dense and pleasurable, offering repletion: "Shall never sweeter Summer feast her fill / Of roses with the nightingales they hear?" Through this implied comparison of her own possibilities with the certain renewal of summer, the speaker offers intense stimulation and gratification. The argument is, of course, fundamentally unsound, because the analogy between seasonal and mortal renewal is false.

In the sestet, which is a stylistic departure from the octave, the speaker tries a different approach. Dropping the dense natural imagery of the octave and appealing to the indifferent man in the limpid, conversational language that Rossetti used so successfully in the *Monna Innominata* sonnet sequence and other later sonnets, the speaker reshapes the situation by hypothetically reversing the roles of the two principals:

> If you had loved me, I not loving you,
>   If you had urged me with the tender plea
> Of what our unknown years to come might do
> (Eternal years, if Time should count too few),
>   I would have owned the point you pressed on me,
>   Was possible, or probable, or true.
>
> (C, II: 102)

This proposition is obviously weighted in the speaker's favor. First, she widens the time frame: in the man's position, the speaker would have "Eternal years, if Time should count too few." And second, she would admit that her feelings could change. But the second point is biased; loving the man as she does, she cannot possibly imagine being cold toward him. It proves nothing for her to say her putative indifference could become love.

While the speaker's arguments are not reasonable, her method is skillful. The final line of the sonnet, with its gradual movement from possibility to truth—"Was possible, or probable, or true"—deftly recapitulates the speaker's incremental method of argument throughout the poem: it begins with a seemingly weak proposition (the whole of the first quatrain; the reference to spring in the second) but becomes increasingly complicated (the depiction of refulgent summer in the second quatrain; the entire sestet). Although the poem's final scenario is unlikely, it suits the speaker's purposes well, for it transforms the current situation into one of mutual love, puts the speaker in control (if only in fantasy), and allows her to escape the imponderable implications of "never" (a word that tolls throughout the octave, but not once in the sestet).

Related to the poems that reverse an unhappy situation through fantasy are those that restructure experience through dreams. The speakers of "The Dream" (1847), "Two Parted" (1853), "Echo" (1854), and the fourth sonnet of the *Monna Innominata* sequence, for example, reformulate an unhappy relationship into a "joy-dream" ("The Dream," l. 29). In a few notable poems, Rossetti uses the dream strategy to rather different ends. In the sonnet "On The Wing" (1862), for example, in which a doomed relationship is portrayed through the symbolism of the speaker's dream, Rossetti uses the dream, not to rewrite the script, but to distance it. Although Rossetti frequently wrote about failed love, she rarely focused on a relationship's dissolution. It is as if she could not write directly or at length about this powerful source of her poetry, or bear to represent it unmitigated by the transforming functions of memory, fantasy, or dream. To dwell on pure loss was virtually impossible for her. In "On the Wing," the failure of love can only be represented on a plane multiply recessed from reality.

> Once in a dream (for once I dreamed of you)
>> We stood together in an open field;
>> Above our heads two swift-winged pigeons wheeled,
> Sporting at ease and courting full in view.
> When loftier still a broadening darkness flew,
>> Down-swooping, and a ravenous hawk revealed;
>> Too weak to fight, to fond to fly, they yield;

So farewell life and love and pleasures new.
Then as their plumes fell fluttering to the ground,
　Their snow-white plumage flecked with crimson drops,
　　I wept, and thought I turned towards you to weep:
　　But you were gone; while rustling hedgerow tops
　Bent in a wind which bore to me a sound
　　Of far-off piteous bleat of lambs and sheep.

(C, I: 138)

The sonnet consists of three layers of experience: first, the speaker's narration of the dream to an unspecified listener; second, the events of the dream itself—the activities of the pigeons and the hawk, the companion's disappearance, etc.; and third, the layer most recessed from actual experience, the symbolic significance of the dream's central action—the hawk's destruction of the pigeons. The fate of the pigeons stands for the doomed relationship between the speaker and her companion in the dream. Rossetti has chosen to represent this fate at multiple removes from reality: it is the signification of a symbol within a dream within a narrative of a dream within a poem. Apparently, the speaker cannot bear to get any closer to the subject of love's failure. At the end of the poem, she does move one step nearer—from the level of symbol back to her narration of the dream—allowing us to see how the pigeons' example applies to this relationship: "I wept, and thought I turned towards you to weep: / But you were gone." But this is as close as she can get to representing the painful failure. It is an ominous, hopeless poem, as the bleak imagery of the final lines confirms: "while rustling hedgerow tops / Bent in a wind which bore to me a sound / Of far-off piteous bleat of lambs and sheep." But the hopelessness remains separated from the speaker's actual experience through the distancing strategy of the dream.

Throughout her career, Rossetti's need to distance and immobilize the dangerous unpredictabilities of love was also well served by the transforming strategy of anticipation. As with remembering and fantasizing, anticipating the renewal of a broken love affair was a way to mitigate loss and to create new versions of experience. In the poems about lovers' separations in which anticipation operates, the speaker hopes for a perfect reunion, not in this life, but in Heaven. Anticipation and memory are often used within the same poem. It is as if the speaker realizes that remembered love, while enormously comforting, is, finally, hopeless because it has no future. So, increasingly, her eyes become fixed, not on "all that was in the long ago" ("An End"), but on all that might be in the future. The final stanza of "Memory" demonstrates this transition:

> But often in my worn life's autumn weather
> I watch there with clear eyes,
> And think how it will be in Paradise
> When we're together.
>
> (C, I: 148)

And in "Echo" (1854), a lovely and poignant lyric about remembered love, the speaker moves from memory to dream to hope in her attempt to salvage something from her loss:

> Oh dream how sweet, too sweet, too bitter sweet,
> Whose wakening should have been in Paradise,
> Where souls brimfull of love abide and meet;
> Where thirsting longing eyes
> Watch the slow door
> That opening, letting in, lets out no more.
>
> (C, I: 46)

As these lines suggest, Rossetti's vision of Heaven was a very personal one, conceived, among other things, as the best locus for unmistakably romantic relationships. One of the reasons for the difficulty of separating her "general" (William Michael Rossetti's term) poems from her devotional ones is this conflation of the idea of a Christian Heaven with a lovers' Paradise. Indeed, in many of the later poems the lover whom the speaker hopes to meet in the romantic Paradise merges with a loving Christ figure awaiting her arrival in Heaven.

The 1858 poem "The Convent Threshold" is both a provocative example of the uses to which Rossetti put the distancing, idealizing properties of anticipation and an important summary of the other postures she habitually adopted toward the failure of love. From a broad perspective, the poem duplicates the dramatic pattern of many other poems in the failed-love group: A speaker reacts to a broken relationship by dedicating herself to an abstract vision of love, which she hopes will one day be realized in Heaven. As is so often the case, there is no clear explanation of the speaker's decision to terminate the relationship; we are told only that it has something to do with family rivalries and unspecified guilt:

> There's blood between us, love, my love,
> There's father's blood, there's brother's blood;
> And blood's a bar I cannot pass:
> . . . .
> My lily feet are soiled with mud,
> With scarlet mud which tells a tale
> Of hope that was, of guilt that was,
> Of love that shall not yet avail;
>
> (C, I: 61, 62)

Overcome with grief and guilt, the speaker decides to enter a convent, repent, and set her eyes on Heaven. But though she leaves her lover, she does not forget their relationship; it will remain the center of her life. She wants to be cleansed of her guilt, but not of her love. She hopes to gain a purified and perfected heavenly love, a version that is free of the stains of mortality like those plaguing the relationships in "Amor Mundi" and "Goblin Market."

Elements of both "Goblin Market" and "Amor Mundi" are heard in "The Convent Threshold." In the "Convent" speaker's rendering of the world to which her lover is unfortunately attracted, we hear the unmistakable tramp of goblin feet: "Milk-white, wine-flushed among the vines, / Up and down leaping, to and fro, / . . . Young men and women come and go." And the reference to the lovers' "sin" in "The Convent Threshold"—"Woe's me that easy way we went, / So rugged when I would return!"—anticipates the final line of "Amor Mundi": "'This downhill path is easy, but there's no turning back.'"

In "The Convent Threshold," the speaker's hope for a heavenly reunion with her lover (which can only be achieved if he, too, repents—apparently an uncertain prospect) is yet another statement of Rossetti's preoccupation with re-formation and perfection. Permanent, blessed, and mutual, such a relationship *is* Paradise. Without it, as the speaker admits (in lines 69 through 79), even Heaven would be lacking. The poem restates Rossetti's fundamental imperative: out of the failure and uncertainty of love must come its perfection.

> When once the morning star shall rise,
> When earth with shadow flees away
> And we stand safe within the door,
> Then you shall lift the veil thereof [from my face].

> Look up, rise up: for far above
> Our palms are grown, our place is set;
> There we shall meet as once we met
> And love with old familiar love.
>
> (C, I: 65)

That the failure of love is immediately, as well as ultimately, productive is demonstrated by the speaker's overwrought, but creative, reaction to her decision to leave her lover. The decision unleashes a torrent of visions: two chillingly detailed, but very different, dreams (ll. 38–109 and 110–25); three visions of Paradise (ll. 17–29, 69–76, and 137–48); and a densely imagistic perception of the world (ll. 31–37). All the transforming strategies have been tapped by this tragedy.

Out of all these distancing and transforming strategies—memory, fantasy, dream, anticipation—issues something that does not exist at the beginning of the poem but is born out of the speaker's attempt to manage her loss. These poems begin in deprivation, but they end in creation. Most obviously, a poem emerges, but within these poems, there is further creativity. In "Memory," for example, the speaker constructs another (virtual) artifact out of her sorrow—not only the poem, but also that unmoving, private room:

> I have a room whereinto no one enters
> Save I myself alone:
> There sits a blessed memory on a throne,
> There my life centres.

In "On the Wing," "Death's Chill Between," and "Touching 'Never,'" entirely new versions of experience are made.

Nowhere are the positive, creative implications of failed love more apparent than in Rossetti's ballads of the 1850s and 1860s; in many, the central problem is a lovers' triangle—usually two women and a man. In these poems, which present named characters and precise dramatic situations, thus fictionalizing or dramatizing the failure of love, the woman's initial loss is frequently the basis for the discovery of a much more important gain. As different as the ballads seem to be from Rossetti's religious poetry, they document a process of discovery similar to the spiritual recovery contained in many of the religious poems. The central women of the ballads reach fundamental truths about themselves that would have been inaccessible without the experience and narration of their loss. Similarly, in many of the religious poems, the speakers' initial descriptions of their spiritual despair become the vehicles by which they discover (or recover) their faith.

The 1859 ballad "Cousin Kate" (originally titled "Up and Down") is a fairly straightforward example of the pattern of gain through loss. The speaker's story of seduction and rejection is told to her cousin Kate—the woman her former lover has married. The speaker's reaction to her rejection by the "great lord" is decidedly mixed. She is unquestionably jealous and ashamed:

> The neighbours call you good and pure,
>   Call me an outcast thing.
> Even so I sit and howl in dust,
>   You sit in gold and sing.
>
> (C, I: 32)

Yet this jealousy does not spring as much from her love of the lord (she never claims she loves him) as it does from her shame about having been the lover of a man who did not marry her and her disappointment over Kate's disloyalty to her. In a manner anticipatory of "Touching 'Never,'" the speaker reveals her own strength and constancy by hypothetically reversing the roles of the two women:

> O cousin Kate, my love was true,
>   Your love was writ in sand:
> If he had fooled not me but you,
>   If you stood where I stand,
> He'd not have won me with his love
>   Nor bought me with his land;
> I would have spit into his face
>   And not have taken his hand.
>
> (C, I: 32)

The love to which she refers in the first two lines of this stanza is not the women's love for the man but their love for each other. The speaker is actually betrayed twice in this poem—by the "great lord," who came to favor her cousin, and by Cousin Kate herself. For the speaker, her cousin's action is the more difficult to bear. But, despite the pain they cause, the betrayals enable the speaker to discover her own strengths: loyalty, constancy, and indifference to wealth. And as the final stanza reveals, the speaker has gained a still-more-tangible gift from her "shameless shameful life" with the man: she has had his son ("My fair-haired son, my shame, my pride"), a gift she realizes her cousin is "not like to get." As in the lyrics, much has come from a failed relationship.

"Cousin Kate" reveals, through its language, much about the dynamics of the male-female relationship. The speaker's words show that she was the passive recipient of her lover's actions. His dominating treatment gave her no opportunity for choice or initiative or self-determination.

> Why did a great lord find me out,
> And praise my flaxen hair?
> Why did a great lord find me out
> To fill my heart with care?
>
> He lured me to his palace home—
> Woe's me for joy thereof—
> To lead a shameless shameful life,
> His plaything and his love.
> He wore me like a silken knot,
> He changed me like a glove.
>
> (C, I: 32)

Throughout this entire passage, the speaker is not the subject of a single active verb. She is no more to this man than an object, a bauble. Nor are there any signs that Cousin Kate can expect anything different:

> O Lady Kate, my cousin Kate,
> You grew more fair than I:
> He saw you at your father's gate,
> Chose you, and cast me by.
> He watched your steps along the lane
> Your work among the rye;
> He lifted you from mean estate
> To sit with him on high.
>
> Because you were so good and pure
> He bound you with his ring.
>
> (C, I: 32)

The language here is reminiscent of the 1849 sonnet "Remember," where the woman could only escape being (quite literally) the *object* of a man's affections by dying. Here, another woman involved in a loveless relationship is luckier: her rejection, while clearly painful, is also an emancipation, enabling or requiring her to develop pride and self-determination.

The longer ballad "Brandons Both," though technically rather awkward and uneven, is important for its repetition of this pattern of gain from loss. In "Brandons Both" (date of composition unknown; first published in 1881), the narrative line is tamer, less sexually suggestive than in "Cousin Kate." Milly Brandon, the central figure of the poem, secretly loves her cousin, Walter Brandon, who in turn, while attracted to Milly, loves and plans to marry Nelly Knollys. Although there is no suggestion of a sexual relationship between the two Brandons, Milly, like the speaker of "Cousin Kate," nurses a secret care:

> Oh fair Milly Brandon, a young maid, a fair maid!
> All her curls are yellow and her eyes are blue,
> And her cheeks were rosy red till a secret care made
> Hollow whiteness of their brightness as a care will do.
>
> (C, II: 102)

In this case, the care is, not the shame of a sexual relationship, but Milly's secret and unreciprocated love for Walter. Hinted at throughout the poem, the secret is not disclosed until the end. As Walter prepares to leave for a hunting trip (whether for animals or women is left ambiguous by the language: "'I shall speed well enough be it hunting or hawking, / Or casting a bait toward the shyest daintiest fin'"), Milly admits her feelings by asking him to wear her rose:

> "Here's a thorny rose: will you wear it an hour,
> Till the petals drop apart still fresh and pink and sweet?
> Till the petals drop from the drooping perished flower,
> And only the graceless thorns are left of it."
>
> (C, II: 104)

Walter understands the significance of the rose but rejects Milly's offer because he loves Nelly Knollys: "I have another rose sprung in another garden, / Another rose which sweetens all the world for me." Unlike the speaker of "Cousin Kate," Milly does not have a child to comfort her, but

Walter's rejection does not leave her comfortless or powerless. The final stanza is an unmistakable statement of self-affirmation:

> "Good-bye, Walter. I can guess which thornless rose you covet;
> Long may it bloom and prolong its sunny morn:
> Yet as for my one thorny rose, I do not cease to love it,
> And if it is no more a flower I love it as a thorn."
>
> (C, II: 105)

Walter's rejection has enabled Milly to discover that she has value and is worthy of self-love. Despite Walter's earlier claim that "nothing comes of nothing," something very precious (Milly's self-ratification) does come from nothing (the failure of her relationship with Walter).

The statement at the end of "Brandons Both" echoes the ending of the long and, for its time, controversial poem "'The Iniquity of the Fathers Upon the Children'" (1865), in which the speaker, an illegitimate child, concludes that she will never marry:

> I think my mind is fixed
> On one point and made up:
> To accept my lot unmixed;
> Never to drug the cup
> But drink it by myself.
> I'll not be wooed for pelf;
> I'll not blot out my shame
> With any man's good name;
> But nameless as I stand,
> My hand is my own hand,
> And nameless as I came
> I go to the dark land.
>
> (C, I: 178)

In both cases, self-discovery and autonomy have resulted from unhappy romances, though in "'The Iniquity,'" the relationship is one generation removed.

According to Lona Mosk Packer, Dante Gabriel Rossetti "objected to both subject and treatment [in "'The Iniquity'"], advising Christina not to include the poem in her 1866 volume." Christina defended her treatment of the topic of illegitimacy in a letter to her brother:

[W]hilst I endorse your opinion of the unavoidable and indeed much-to-be desired unreality of women's work on many social matters, I yet incline to include within the female range such an attempt as this. . . . Moreover, the sketch only gives the girl's own deductions, feelings and semi-resolutions; granted such premises as hers, and right or wrong it seems to me she might easily arrive at such conclusions: and whilst it may truly be urged that unless white could be black and Heaven Hell my experience (thank God) precludes me from hers, I yet don't see why the "Poet mind" should be less able to construct her from its own inner consciousness than a hundred other unknown quantities.[7]

"Cousin Kate" and "Brandons Both" are examples of Christina Rossetti's transforming impulse at its most productive: these ballads construct positive gain out of pain and deprivation. But they also represent an important departure from poems like "Heart's Chill Between," "An End," and "Memory," which altered reality and allowed the troubled speakers to hide from the truth. In the ballads (and in " 'The Iniquity of the Fathers Upon the Children' "), the creativity born of loss provides, not a refuge from the truth, but a means for discovering a deeper, invaluable truth about the speaker's own power and worth. These poems anticipate "Goblin Market" and the later religious poems, in which positive truth issues from loss and uncertainty.

The works discussed in this chapter—poems as seemingly different as "Memory," "Touching 'Never,' " and "Brandons Both"—reenact the central pattern of Rossetti's own life: out of singleness, whether voluntary or imposed, comes creativity, independence, and self-determination. Had Christina Rossetti, at the age of eighteen, married James Collinson (a man with neither resources nor expectations), she almost certainly could not have dedicated her life to poetry. Whether she realized this and refused Collinson as much on these grounds as on religious ones, or whether she was indifferent to the man, we can never know. But an unraveling of motivations is less important than the reverberating truth that Rossetti's career, independence, and self-determination grew out of (and probably in her later life contributed to) the lack of a long-term romantic relationship. Significantly, the year 1849 marked Rossetti's rupture with Collinson and the composition of some of her best poems: "Remember," "An End," "After Death," and "Song" ("Oh roses for the flush of youth"). For Rossetti and the

7. Packer, *Christina Rossetti,* 154.

speakers of her poems, solitude allowed, indeed required, alternative creations. For Rossetti, the creations were poetry and autonomy; for the speakers of her poems, the creations were dreams, fantasies, hopes, memories, self-love, personal strength.

The frequency with which Rossetti re-created this pattern of her own life gives us further insight into the strength of her professional commitment. For Rossetti, poetry was doubly magic: it transformed the mediocre into the wonderful, and more personally, it was the creative restitution born of a deprivation (whether chosen or imposed) that clearly represented a significant loss. The passionate professional commitment evident in Rossetti's letters and in such poems as "A Pause of Thought" undoubtedly originated in Rossetti's understanding of the restitutive function of her poetry. As we see in so many of the poems, her anomalous and obviously painful situation was tolerable, even preferable to many others, as long as she could create something from it. The situation became intolerable only when it refused to be reshaped, leaving the poet with the equally unsatisfactory recourses of expressing the pain (as in "Heart's Chill Between") or of expressing nothing at all (as in "Cobwebs").

While the works discussed in this chapter reveal poetry's great appeal for Rossetti, we must remember that there was much about the creative act that she found disturbing. Writing poetry could transform pain and uncover truth, but it also possessed frightening capabilities. First, by opening up multiple interpretive possibilities, it questioned the existence of a single, stable system by which the world could be decoded. Second, the creative act itself, by arousing and liberating the imagination and the subconscious, threatened Christina Rossetti the strict Anglo-Catholic. And finally, as we saw in "In An Artist's Studio" and elsewhere, the creative act or attitude endangered real experience and the artist's relationship to it. The strenuous personal conflict growing out of such discoveries about the function of art would impel Rossetti to develop a reconciling aesthetic theory—one that could mitigate her ambivalence and justify her choice of career. The most important expression of this aesthetic is the brilliant "Goblin Market" (1859), Rossetti's masterly representation of the function and requirements of poetry.

FOUR

"Goblin Market": A Reconciling Poetic

he best known and most widely discussed of all Christina
Rossetti's poems is "Goblin Market," written in 1859. Although Rossetti herself claimed she "did not mean anything profound by
this fairy tale," readers have ignored this probably disingenuous statement, forwarding a remarkable number and variety of analyses of the
poem. Despite his sister's disclaimer about the meaning of "Goblin Market," William Michael Rossetti realized that "different minds may be
likely to read different messages into [the poem]."[1] His prediction has
proved to be accurate, though perhaps understated. Even before the last
decade's revival of critical interest in Christina Rossetti, a number of
widely divergent and persuasive readings of "Goblin Market" had been
proposed, ranging from the strictly biographical to the religious to the
psychoanalytical.[2] Since 1976, critics have offered even more interpreta-
tions. Ellen Moers, writing in 1976, suggested that the central goblin
experience originated in "fantasies derived from the night side of the
Victorian nursery—a world where childish cruelty and childish sexuality
came to the fore"; Jerome McGann and Miriam Sagan read the poem as,
among other things, a feminist declaration of independence from the

1. William Michael Rossetti (ed.), *Poetical Works of Christina Georgina Rossetti*,
"Notes," 459.

2. Lona Mosk Packer, "Symbol and Reality in Christina Rossetti's *Goblin Mar-
ket*," *Publications of the Modern Language Association*, LXXIII (1958), 375–85; James
Ashcroft Noble, *Impressions and Memories* (London, 1895), 59; Ellen Golub, "Untying
Goblin Apron Strings: A Psychoanalytic Reading of 'Goblin Market,'" *Literature and
Psychology*, XXV (1975), 158–65.

masculine world; and William Going finds in "Goblin Market" a representation of Christina Rossetti's relationship with the members of the Pre-Raphaelite Brotherhood.[3]

For all the "different messages" suggested by the body of the poem, the final 6 lines (of a total of 567 lines), with their firmly insistent moral that "there is no friend like a sister," have led some critics to conclude that Rossetti's intention with "Goblin Market" was to write a poem about the primacy of love and sacrifice over any other experience or value. For many, the intransigence of the poem's concluding message, coming in the wake of 561 lines of rich ambiguity, has been frustrating and disappointing. Writing in 1933, B. Ifor Evans remarked on the "theme and movement [of 'Goblin Market'], suggesting many things and not assignable to one source" and the "concluding moral acting as an anticlimax to the glamour and magic which precede it." Nearly forty years later, Stuart Curran was troubled by the same contradiction: "The powerful implications of this fable of sensual possession are resolved into a panegyric for sisterly love, and what begins as a startling complement to Poe and Baudelaire settles stiffly into a Victorian parlor."[4]

It is a mistake, however, to see the concluding insertion of didacticism as an eleventh-hour retreat from the earlier wildness of the poem, as a timid woman's flight from the sensuous gratifications in which Laura has reveled. The concluding six lines are not a tacked-on apology to the demands of Victorian decorum or the means by which the poet eased her own discomfort with the frightening implications of the first part of the poem; rather, they are absolutely necessary to complete the definition the poem has been in the process of making since the first line. Among the many other things that Christina Rossetti is undertaking in "Goblin Market" is a detailed definition of her own poetics—of her understanding of the components of poetry itself and the activity that goes into

3. Ellen Moers, *Literary Women: The Great Writers* (Garden City, N.Y., 1976), 105; McGann, "Christina Rossetti's Poems: A New Edition and a Revaluation"; Sagan, "Christina Rossetti's 'Goblin Market' and Feminist Literary Criticism"; William T. Going, "'Goblin Market' and the Pre-Raphaelite Brotherhood," *Pre-Raphaelite Review,* III (1979), 54–62.

4. B. Ifor Evans, "The Sources of Christina Rossetti's 'Goblin Market,' " *Modern Language Review,* XXVIII (1933), 161; Stuart Curran, "The Lyric Voice of Christina Rossetti," *Victorian Poetry,* IX (1971), 288.

its creation. Without the final six lines, that definition would remain unfinished.

The subject of poetry was not a new focus for Rossetti; she examined it carefully in a number of earlier poems. But "Goblin Market" was unquestionably the most extended presentation of the aesthetic theory Rossetti had been developing, refining, and testing for at least ten years, since her first treatment of the subject in "A Pause of Thought" (1848).[5]

The dramatic situation of "Goblin Market" is by now familiar: A young single woman, impelled by her curiosity and need for excitement, is drawn into an experience that initially promises change and gratification but finally endangers her life. In this case, the experience is not with one man but with a group of men—strange, goblin men. As in the earlier poem "Repining," the woman escapes the dangers raised by her experience, regains her innocence, and returns happily and gratefully to her life of serene domesticity. But, despite the similarities in plot between "Goblin Market" and "Repining," "The Lowest Room," and "The Heart Knoweth Its Own Bitterness," a number of significant features distinguish the later poem from its predecessors.

The first difference is in the nature of the central experience. The lengthy journeys that the women of "Moonshine" and "Amor Mundi" make with a man signify long-term sexual relationships—a kind of marriage. Many elements document this reading: the metaphor of the journey, the unmistakable sexuality of the men (the "love-locks" of "Amor Mundi" and the hand-holding of "Moonshine"), the proposal and exchange of vows in "Moonshine." Given these details, we can assume that these relationships include a sexual component, but Rossetti is not explicit on the subject. It is not sex but the deceit and the permanence of the alliances that endanger the women. But Laura's experience—we can hardly call it a relationship—with the goblin men is far from long-term or romantic, though it has obvious sexual overtones. For one thing, she is trafficking with *men,* not with a single man. For another, the experience is anything but permanent—its transience almost kills Laura. And finally, unlike her predecessors, Laura gains tremendous, albeit temporary, sensual gratification from her experience with men—she is the only such

5.   See McGann, "Christina Rossetti's Poems: A New Edition and a Revaluation"; Gilbert and Gubar, *The Madwoman in the Attic,* 564–75; and A. A. DeVitis, "'Goblin Market': Fairy Tale and Reality," *Journal of Popular Culture,* I (1968), 418–26.

gratified woman in the Rossetti canon (with the exception of the speaker in "A Birthday"). Laura's goblin adventure, whatever it represents, is only distantly related to the experiences of the women in "Moonshine," "Amor Mundi," "Repining," and "The Heart Knoweth Its Own Bitterness."

A second critical feature distinguishing "Goblin Market" from these earlier works is the nature of Laura's ultimate relationship to the action of the poem. The difference is a simple one, but in it we are given the clue by which to read Rossetti's poetic theory. Although Laura is unmistakably reminiscent of the women speakers of "The Lowest Room" and "The Heart Knoweth Its Own Bitterness" and of the central women characters in "Repining," "Moonshine," and "Amor Mundi," she is the only story-teller, the only one of this group who relates her own story, retrospectively, to others. In "The Lowest Room," the speaker does narrate her recollection of the earlier conversation with her sister, but she does not present a carefully shaped story for the edification or entertainment of others, as Laura does for her and Lizzie's children at the end of "Goblin Market." In "Goblin Market," there are actually two storytellers, or poets: the narrator of the action, in whose all-encompassing voice the entire poem is spoken; and Laura herself, who, at the end of "Goblin Market," tells her story (condensed and paraphrased) through the narrator and adds, in her own voice, the concluding moral about sisterhood. Laura's role as storyteller enables us, requires us to ask this critical question of the poem: What are the elements in this goblin experience, or set of goblin experiences (Laura's and Lizzie's), that allow it to become poetry? Or, put a bit differently, what is it about the experiences in this poem that makes Laura a poet? The answers, which are contained in "Goblin Market," serve as a full explanation of Christina Rossetti's poetic theory.

"Goblin Market" is further distinguished from earlier, related poems—indeed, from virtually everything else Rossetti wrote—by its style. If Rossetti was predicting the quality of her poetic manner in "An End," where she wrote "To few chords and sad and low / Sing we so," "Goblin Market" marks a significant departure from her plan. With its metrical unpredictability, its wildly proliferating imagery, its abundant store of language, "Goblin Market" is unique in the Rossetti canon. More than any other element of the poem, the style itself brilliantly reveals Rossetti's strained ambivalence about creative activity.

The poem's stylistic elements create the impression that "Goblin Market" was an enjoyable poem to write; we certainly enjoy reading it. Much of the poem's magnetic appeal and artistic success derive from this impression. First, there is the way the poem sounds. When read aloud, the tumbling variety and irregularity of meter engage and astound the ear. John Ruskin, who came to think better of Christina Rossetti's verse, was initially offended by the seeming formlessness of the poem, by its lack of metrical discipline. To Dante Gabriel Rossetti he wrote, "Your sister should exercise herself in the severest commonplace of meter until she can write as the public likes; then if she puts in her observation and passion all will become precious. But she must have Form first."[6] Christina Rossetti could, of course, write strictly formal poetry, but "Goblin Market" is unlike the many Rossetti poems ("Amor Mundi," for instance) that studiously adhere to a complex metrical pattern. Throughout the poem, trochee, dactyl, and iamb follow each other with apparently indiscriminate abandon while line length expands and contracts with whimsical irregularity:

> Evening by evening
> Among the brookside rushes,
> Laura bowed her head to hear,
> Lizzie veiled her blushes:
> Crowding close together
> In the cooling weather
> With clasping arms and cautioning lips
> With tingling cheeks and finger tips.
>
> (C, I: 12)

In "Goblin Market," Rossetti has called upon her talents as a writer of nursery rhymes and children's verse to produce a delightfully hypnotic metrical effect.

> "One hauls a basket,
> One bears a plate,
> One lugs a golden dish
> Of many pounds weight."
>
> (C, I: 12)

The meter of these lines exactly corresponds to that of the sheep's reply in "Baa-Baa, Black Sheep" while the following lines are reminiscent of

---

6. Doughty and Wahl (eds.), *Letters of Dante Gabriel Rossetti,* II, 391.

"Jack, Be Nimble" or many of Rossetti's own nursery rhymes (like "Angels at the foot" or "If a mouse could fly" from her 1872 *Sing-Song: A Nursery Rhyme Book*).

> "Figs to fill your mouth,
> Citrons from the South,
> Sweet to tongue and sound to eye;
> Come buy, come buy."
>
> (C, I: 11–12)

While the subject and implications of "Goblin Market" are certainly not proper for a children's poem, there is no denying that the work sounds like one.[7] When Alexander Macmillan read the poem to a men's club, the listeners immediately reacted to the poem's childlike quality. According to Macmillan, "They seemed at first to wonder whether I was making fun of them; by degrees they got as still as death, and when I finished there was a tremendous burst of applause."[8]

The sheer excess of the poem—particularly the ceaseless variety and fecundity of its language—is also compelling. Like the soil that feeds the roots of the goblins' fruit trees, the narrating poet's mind is endlessly fertile. Despite the tremendous demands made upon her vocabulary by the poem's lengthy catalogs, her supply is endless. As the opening list of the goblins' fruits demonstrates, Rossetti is never at a loss for words—nor does one word ever seem forced or inappropriate:

> "Apples and quinces,
> Lemons and oranges,
> Plump unpecked cherries,
> Melons and raspberries,
> Bloom-down-cheeked peaches,
> Swart-headed mulberries,
> Wild free-born cranberries,
> Crab-apples, dewberries,
> Pine-apples, blackberries,
> Apricots, strawberries."
>
> (C, I: 11)

7. Sagan, "Christina Rossetti's 'Goblin Market' and Feminist Literary Criticism," 69.

8. George A. Macmillan (ed.), *Letters of Alexander Macmillan* (Glasgow, 1908), 94–95.

Rossetti's arrangement of this catalog of fruits into rhythmical poetic lines with striking occurrences of alliteration and assonance is skillful. In light of Rossetti's characteristic poetical mode of working within rigid restrictions, this verbal excess is surprising. Instead of the economy employed in such poems as "Downcast" and "Of My Life," "Goblin Market" relies on a kind of profligacy of words.

This verbal fecundity does not characterize all the voices of the poem all the time; only the narrator consistently uses language in this way, presenting the action of the poem with this air of intoxicated exuberance. Permeating the verse is a sense of the poet's breathless inebriation with the process of writing. The proliferation of words, rhythms, metaphors, and similes suggests an artist reveling in her creativity, whose love of her craft, like Laura's love of the fruit, is insatiable. In the following lines describing Laura's frenzied reaction to the antidote, as simile breeds simile in Homeric fashion, it appears that the poet cannot get enough of the creative process.

> Her locks streamed like the torch
> Borne by a racer at full speed,
> Or like the mane of horses in their flight,
> Or like an eagle when she stems the light
> Straight toward the sun,
> Or like a caged thing freed,
> Or like a flying flag when armies run.
>
> (C, I: 24)

Similar in effect is the passage in which Lizzie withstands the goblins:

> White and golden Lizzie stood,
> Like a lily in a flood,—
> Like a rock of blue-veined stone
> Lashed by tides obstreperously,—
> Like a beacon left alone
> In a hoary roaring sea,
> Sending up a golden fire,—
> Like a fruit-crowned orange-tree,
> White with blossoms honey-sweet,
> Sore beset by wasp and bee,—
> Like a royal virgin town

> Topped with gilded dome and spire
> Close beleaguered by a fleet
> Mad to tug her standard down.
>
> (C, I: 22)

The exuberant, joyful tone of the narrator's language seems at times strikingly incongruous to the actions being related, as if the poet is oblivious to the implications of the violence and suffering in the poem. The passage containing what is essentially the goblins' rape of Lizzie after she has refused to eat their fruits (ll. 395–437) is as stylistically childlike and inconsequential as are any of the more innocent passages of the poem:

> Lashing their tails
> They trod and hustled her.
> Elbowed and jostled her,
> Clawed with their nails,
> Barking, mewing, hissing, mocking,
> Tore her gown and soiled her stocking,
> Twitched her hair out by the roots,
> Stamped upon her tender feet,
> Held her hands and squeezed their fruits
> Against her mouth to make her eat.
>
> (C, I: 21)

The action described in these lines is quite brutal, but the *sound* of the lines is playful and merry.

Whatever the meaning of "Goblin Market," its prolixity of language and imagery, its childlike tone and sound leave the reader with the impression of a writer carried away by sheer delight in the tools of her craft. In short, the style of the majority of the poem represents all that is hedonistic, intoxicating, and irresponsible in the creative process—all that comes most easily to the poet. In the many long strings of similes, for example, particularly the early ones, it is as if Rossetti is saying, "Look, I can make all these beautiful images, but I don't have to choose among them; I can simply revel in my skill." But while the easy, delightful parts of writing poetry give Rossetti much joy, they are also a source of considerable consternation—not only, as we might expect, because she finds any immediate gratification suspect but also because she thinks they do not suffice for fully developed poetry.

The narrator's apparent enchantment or intoxication with the tools of her art allies her with the wayward Laura, who experiences a comparable inebriation with the goblins' beautiful, abundant fruit. In Laura, Rossetti has produced a natural poet-figure—a character possessing all the impulses and instincts necessary, though not always sufficient, for the creation of art. First, Laura is curious; indeed, it is her curiosity, not her yearning for sensual pleasures, that initially attracts her to the goblins. At the opening of the poem, Laura warns Lizzie:

> "Lie close," Laura said,
> Pricking up her golden head:
> "We must not look at goblin men,
> We must not buy their fruits:
> Who knows upon what soil they fed
> Their hungry thirsty roots?"
>
> (C, I: 12)

Here, and a few lines later, Laura admits to a fascination with the origin of the goblins' gorgeous fruits:

> "How fair the vine must grow
> Whose grapes are so luscious;
> How warm the wind must blow
> Thro' those fruit bushes."
>
> (C, I: 12)

In her speculative depiction of the faraway land of the fruits' cultivation, Laura displays the artist's ability to envision the unknown or the unseen. She, much like the maker of the poem in which she figures, is instinctively impelled to give form and reality to a land that she has never seen but that, for some reason, has become important in her imagination.

Laura's poetic language further demonstrates her artistic bent. During the first half of the poem, her speeches are filled with vivid, carefully detailed descriptions. When finally persuaded to eat the fruits, for example, Laura laments her insolvency in a beautiful image:

> "And all my gold is on the furze
> That shakes in windy weather
> Above the rusty heather."
>
> (C, I: 14)

And having partaken of the wonderful feast, she recreates her experience for Lizzie in one of the most sensually vivid and aurally pleasing passages of the poem:

> "You cannot think what figs
> My teeth have met in,
> What melons icy-cold
> Piled on a dish of gold
> Too huge for me to hold,
> What peaches with a velvet nap,
> Pellucid grapes without one seed:
> Odorous indeed must be the mead
> Whereon they grow, and pure the wave they drink
> With lilies at the brink,
> And sugar-sweet their sap."
>
> (C, I: 15–16)

The effective and sophisticated use of alliteration and assonance and the mellifluous choice and placement of words are the marks of a talented poet—a poet enchanted with the dreamlike essences of the imagination.

Lizzie, on the other hand, is lacking in all the qualities so profusely bestowed upon Laura. While Laura's imagination and her fascination with the unknown are immediately stimulated by the goblins, Lizzie's curiosity remains completely untouched:

> "No," said Lizzie: "no, no, no;
> Their offers should not charm us,
> Their evil gifts would harm us."
> She thrust a dimpled finger
> In each ear, shut eyes and ran.
>
> (C, I: 12–13)

Unlike Laura, who "chose to linger, / Wondering at each merchant man," Lizzie refuses to admit any element of the wonderful into her mind. The style and substance of her language are far removed from Laura's poetic speech: Her subsequent admonition about the dangers of goblin men is not only dull and conventional in its cautious tone ("Dear, you should not stay so late, / Twilight is not good for maidens") but stylistically stagnant and prosaic. The passage in which she relates the sad history of Jeanie is similarly deficient in imagination and energy, though it is a good example of the reflection of sense by sound:

> "But ever in the noonlight
> She pined and pined away;
> Sought them [the goblins] by night and day,
> Found them no more, but dwindled and grew grey;
> Then fell with the first snow,
> While to this day no grass will grow
> Where she lies low:
> I planted daisies there a year ago
> That never blow.
> You should not loiter so."
>
> (C, I: 15)

The monotony of the rhyming pattern of these lines and the dearth of any sensually appealing images (the dearth, in fact, of any images whatsoever) demonstrate Lizzie's decidedly nonpoetic vision.

The extent of Lizzie's unobservant, unimaginative attitude toward the world around her is pointedly summarized in the narrator's description of the beginning of Lizzie's search for an antidote to give to Laura.

> Till Laura dwindling
> Seemed knocking at Death's door:
> Then Lizzie weighed no more
> Better and worse;
> But put a silver penny in her purse,
> Kissed Laura, crossed the heath with clumps of furze
> At twilight, halted by the brook:
> *And for the first time in her life*
> *Began to listen and look.*(my emphasis)
>
> (C, I: 19)

In its suggestion of a habitual posture of insensibility to external stimuli, this is a remarkable commentary on Lizzie. Perhaps nowhere in the poem do the scales of the narrator's preference weigh more heavily in Laura's favor. Whether intentionally or not, Rossetti has made Laura the more appealing of the two sisters; for all her seemingly exemplary caution, Lizzie has a good deal of the Philistine about her.

The crux of the poem, the question that has elicited a greater variety of theories than have any others posed about "Goblin Market," is the significançe of the goblin men and their fruits. The strongly sexual, seductive element in the goblins' appeal to Laura has been noted by a number of critics and can hardly be denied.[9] But concentrating on the sexual component—or any other single component of the goblins—limits our understanding of Rossetti's wider purposes. More important than any one interpretation of the goblins is their ambiguity. Their very plurality of meaning (which is particularly emphasized at the beginning of the poem) becomes the key to understanding their function in the poem.

Most broadly, the goblins and their fruits signify the ambiguity, variety, and disorder of fantasy before it is attached to some stable and, for Rossetti, necessarily moral interpretive system. For Rossetti, such random imaginative activity is dangerous if it remains morally indecipherable. The goblins are the perfect representatives of that danger—of the early activity of the imagination, with its undisciplined proliferation of disordered and highly ambiguous creations. This form of fantasy may be a species of creativity—an activity that Rossetti herself found enormously gratifying—but she is firm in her view that it is not art. In order to qualify as art, the creations of the imagination must be put together in a way that makes sense—not just intellectual and aesthetic sense, but moral sense as well. "Goblin Market" is one of the first and most important statements of the view Rossetti develops further in her religious verse: that poetry must operate as an analogue of the ordered, moral universe that was the basis of Anglo-Catholic belief. Poetry can have many layers of meaning, but those meanings must be consistent with, and demonstrative of, a just, Christian universe. As we have seen in "Amor Mundi," multiply suggestive signs, or representations that are free of a clear meaning or contextual system, signal, for reader and poet alike, a destructive chaos that comes too close to the unthinkable conclusion that the world itself is frameless and incoherent. Although the goblins and their fruits are far more developed as symbols than is the meteor in "Amor Mundi," they work in much the same way—as an "undeciphered solemn signal of help or hurt." Laura, like her predecessor in "Amor Mundi," is confronted with unfamiliar phenomena that she cannot or will not decipher correctly. But in "Goblin Market," the fruits are more than an ambiguous portent; they represent the fantastic creations of the imagination before the discovery (or imposi-

9. See, for example, Mermin, "Heroic Sisterhood in 'Goblin Market.'"

tion) of a unifying order and frame. The infinite suggestiveness of these creations makes them extremely potent and attractive, but also slippery, disruptive, and threatening.

In order to identify the function of the goblins in the aesthetic statement made in "Goblin Market," we must recognize just how ambiguous they are. Throughout the poem, Rossetti has taken great care to present the goblins and all that is associated with them as so multifaceted as to be uninterpretable, their real essence finally indeterminate. The only thing we know for sure about the goblins is that they are male. Everything else about them is persistently inconsistent. That they are goblins gives us (and should give Laura) a clue to their evil intent, but beyond that, their "goblinhood" does nothing to clarify their species. When Laura first observes them, she describes them to Lizzie as "little men" (l. 55), but upon closer examination they appear to be as bestial as they are human. As the narrator relates,

> One had a cat's face,
> One whisked a tail,
> One tramped at a rat's pace.
> One crawled like a snail,
> One like a wombat prowled obtuse and furry,
> One like a ratel tumbled hurry skurry.
>
> (C, I: 13)

Elsewhere in the poem, as William Michael Rossetti recognized, "various designations are given to the goblins; they are 'goblin men, little men, merchant men, fruit-merchant men.'" That Christina intended the species of the goblins to be equivocal is demonstrated by her illustrations. According to William Michael, Christina drew in the margins "several of the goblins,—all very slim agile figures in a close-fitting garb of blue; their faces, hands, and feet are sometimes human, sometimes brute-like, but of a scarcely definable type. The only exception is the 'parrot-voiced' goblin who cried 'Pretty goblin.' He is a true parrot (such as Christina could draw one)."[10]

Equally protean are the goblins' voices and manners. Before Laura's encounter with them, the goblin men communicate in lovely, innocent tones:

10. William Michael Rossetti (ed.), *Poetical Works of Christina Georgina Rossetti,* "Notes," 459, 460.

> She [Laura] heard a voice like voice of doves
> Cooing all together:
> They sounded kind and full of loves
> In the pleasant weather.
>
> (C, I: 13)

At times, they are gentle and hospitable, but they can also be "cross-grained, uncivil" (l. 395) and "shrill" (l. 89); they "grunt," "snarl," "bark," and "hiss" (ll. 393–402) when their blandishments are refused. And, more confusing still, the goblins can disappear, as they do for Laura, who desperately wants to repeat her encounter with them. In the goblin men, then, with their contradictory characteristics and behaviors, their multiple appearances, and their resistance to classification and explanation, Rossetti has created a group of totally ambiguous, fantastic creatures— apt representatives of the undisciplined clamorings of the creative imagination.

Nowhere are the variety of their appearance and the confusion about their identity more overwhelming than in the scene of their greeting Lizzie on her errand of mercy. The goblins

> Came towards her hobbling,
> Flying, running, leaping,
> Puffing and blowing,
> Chuckling, clapping, crowing,
> Clucking and gobbling,
> Mopping and mowing,
> Full of airs and graces,
> Pulling wry faces,
> Demure grimaces,
> Cat-like and rat-like,
> Ratel- and wombat-like,
> Snail-paced in a hurry,
> Parrot-voiced and whistler,
> Helter skelter, hurry skurry,
> Chattering like magpies,
> Fluttering like pigeons,
> Gliding like fishes.
>
> (C, I: 19–20)

This passage, especially with the insertion, in the final three lines, of wildlife that has not yet been associated with the goblins, is striking proof of the endless variety and possibility of the goblins. But by this point, knowing as we do the sufferings of Laura and the risks incurred by Lizzie, the goblins' increasing plurality is only menacing. The time for reveling in the abundance and multiplicity of the goblins' offerings has passed; their variety and number have become disturbing and dangerous, threatening to overpower Lizzie completely. In order for this entire goblin experience, with all its seemingly endless possibilities, to become harmless again, it must be unified by a single meaning, or moral, which it will be Lizzie's job to provide.

The multiple implications of the goblin experience are mirrored by the sheer variety and number of the goblins' fruits. In the opening catalog of the poem, the goblins mention sixteen fruits:

> "Apples and quinces,
> Lemons and oranges,
> Plump unpecked cherries,
> Melons and raspberries,
> Bloom-down-cheeked peaches,
> Swart-headed mulberries,
> Wild free-born cranberries,
> Crab-apples, dewberries,
> Pine-apples, blackberries,
> Apricots, strawberries."
>
> (C, I: 11)

Within the next sixteen lines, thirteen additional fruits are added to their inventory. Faced with such abundance and variety, Laura cannot choose among the fruits but, as she tells Lizzie in lines 165 through 183, eats them all. At this point in Laura's experience, there is no possibility of studied choice and thus no possibility of form or meaning.

The similes that represent Laura's succumbing to the goblins' temptations are a masterly reflection of the initial ambiguity of the goblin experience. In some of the most beautiful lines of the poem, the narrator describes Laura's losing struggle:

> Laura stretched her gleaming neck
> Like a rush-imbedded swan,
> Like a lily from the beck,
> Like a moonlit poplar branch,

Like a vessel at the launch
When its last restraint is gone.

(C, I: 13)

One of the earliest of such strings of similes in the poem, this passage is remarkable for the balance it achieves between contradictory implications; it is, finally, noncommittal. Laura's temptation, represented by the stretching of her gleaming neck toward the goblins, is compared to four other phenomena, all straining to break loose from a base. But the connotations of the straining swan, lily, poplar branch, and vessel are not obviously negative, as might be expected by those who have read the poem and know what Laura will suffer. While we might see the release of the lily from the brook and the branch from the poplar tree as harmful (neither can live unattached to its source of nourishment), the escape of the swan from the entangling rushes can only be viewed as positive. The final, more extended image of the vessel at the launch remains poised between a positive and negative interpretation. A vessel freed to brave the open seas could suggest either a desirable liberation from cruel restraint or a dangerous departure from safety and security. Thus, Laura's action, compared as it is to such uncertain and contradictory phenomena, is as ambiguous and unfathomable as are the goblins themselves. She is operating under conditions of infinite possibility and no certainty.

Rossetti often uses simile, particularly a series of similes, to suggest uncertainty or incompletion. As much as the narrator of "Goblin Market" seems to delight in her ability to create endless poetic images, she also asserts that there is something frightening about definition through comparison, as in the passage depicting Laura's temptation. When we do not know what the reality is—in this case, what the actual nature of Laura's action is—the other references (to the swan, the poplar branch, etc.) serve, not as an enriching descriptive method, but as a desperate and hopeless means for defining an essence that is not known. What Laura's experience is like at this point does not tell us what it is; and without that single meaning, her experience is pointless and therefore dangerous. As the significance of the poem's action becomes clearer, these strings of similes become, for the most part, far less ambiguous. Near the end of the poem, for example, Laura's reaction to the antidote procured by Lizzie is presented in a series of five similes, all positive:

> Her locks streamed like the torch
> Borne by a racer at full speed,
> Or like the mane of horses in their flight,
> Or like an eagle when she stems the light
> Straight toward the sun,
> Or like a caged thing freed,
> Or like a flying flag when armies run.
>
> (C, I: 24)

Significantly, the ending of the poem—Laura's own story told to her and Lizzie's children—contains only one simile, and it refers to the duality of the goblins' fruits, to the danger of their initially unrecognizable essence: "Their fruits like honey to the throat / But poison in the blood."

The final simile series of the poem, describing the defeat of Laura's sensual yearnings, is, like the one directly preceding it, internally consistent. All the vehicles are essentially positive. Yet, curiously, the tenor of these similes—Laura's sensual yearnings—is, within the context of the poem, decidedly negative. Ungratified sensuality is undesirable and destructive, yet its defeat is portrayed in terms of the destruction of uniformly *positive* objects.

> Sense failed in the mortal strife:
> Like the watch-tower of a town
> Which an earthquake shatters down,
> Like a lightning-stricken mast,
> Like a wind-uprooted tree
> Spun about,
> Like a foam-topped waterspout
> Cast down headlong in the sea,
> She fell at last.
>
> (C, I: 25)

The essential contradiction between tenor and vehicles in this passage reveals Rossetti's own ambivalence toward the failure of sense "in the mortal strife," her own attraction to the pleasures offered, then cruelly withheld, by the goblins. These lines are Rossetti's quiet admission of the appeal of the goblins' gifts, of the undeniable loss that accompanies the failure of what she refers to as "sense." Although Rossetti cannot endorse an experience like Laura's with the fruits as complete and meaningful, by the end of the poem she will find other ways to express her delight in its possibilities.

Rossetti's insistence on the gender of the goblins and on the sexual aspect of the goblin encounters requires comment. Given the centrality of creativity in Rossetti's own life, it is curious that she should have manufactured these decidedly male goblins to represent the clamorings of fantasy, the undisciplined, incoherent raw materials of art. But within the social system of the poem, her choice is fitting. The poem's central symbol for fantasy had to be as distant as possible from the sisters' innocent, even existence. And what is more obviously removed from the pristine, asexual domesticity of Laura and Lizzie at the opening of the poem than overt male sexuality? The sexual component of Laura's encounter with the goblins also lends it a forbidden quality, which is exactly the point that Rossetti wants to make about the episode: such an encounter is delightful, but if engaged in gratuitously, it is wrong. Laura's experience with the goblins shares something of the quality of the relationships portrayed in "Repining," "Moonshine," and "Amor Mundi." In those poems, Rossetti represented young women's experiences with men as deceptive and destructive. Laura's encounter with the goblins—appropriately male— raises the same dangers: Their apparent harmlessness and generosity turn into a vicious parsimony that almost kills Laura. In Rossetti's poetic world, the variety and intensity that seem to be identified as male principles end up being misleading and ultimately inaccessible. The initial wildness, exciting and perhaps even necessary to the creative process, prevents positive growth and regeneration because of its unreliability. As "Goblin Market" ultimately argues, variety and intensity can yield a meaningful and lasting creation only when they are joined with a stable, moral vision.

It is not until the following evening in the poem, when Laura, who has been "in an absent dream" all day, realizes she can no longer hear the goblins, that we recognize just how destructive her experience has been. The result of her inebriation with the fruits is a hopeless and barren addiction.

> Laura turned cold as stone
> To find her sister heard that cry alone,
> That goblin cry,

"Come buy our fruits, come buy."
Must she then buy no more such dainty fruit?
Must she no more such succous pasture find,
Gone deaf and blind?
Her tree of life drooped from the root:
She said not one word in her heart's sore ache;
But peering thro' the dimness, nought discerning,
Trudged home, her pitcher dripping all the way;
So crept to bed, and lay
Silent till Lizzie slept;
Then sat up in a passionate yearning,
And gnashed her teeth for baulked desire, and wept
As if her heart would break.

(C, I: 17–18)

Laura's situation at this point in the poem is similar to Dante Gabriel
Rossetti's in "In An Artist's Studio." For both, the light of reality has
grown pale beside the addicting intensity of the creative experience. The
domestic routine that had been Laura's life before her introduction to the
goblins is now unbearable to her:

She no more swept the house,
Tended the fowls or cows,
Fetched honey, kneaded cakes of wheat,
Brought water from the brook:
But sat down listless in the chimney-nook
And would not eat.

(C, I: 18–19)

Ironically, nothing can come of the seemingly infinite possibilities of the
experience but sterility and, finally, death. Such was the fate of the unfor-
tunate Jeanie, who

"pined and pined away;
Sought them [the goblins] by night and day,
Found them no more but dwindled and grew grey;
Then fell with the first snow,
While to this day no grass will grow
Where she lies low."

(C, I: 15)

Clearly, the same tragedy would have befallen Laura had it not been for the courageous intervention of Lizzie—an intervention that both saves Laura's life and turns the entire episode into a poem, into a true work of art.

Lizzie's encounter with the goblin men is the critical act of "Goblin Market"; without it, Rossetti could never have written the first half of the poem. While the ambiguity and provocativeness of Laura's goblin experience have elicited more critical discussion, Lizzie's act of braving the goblin men actually receives far more attention in the poem itself than does Laura's adventure. Laura's encounter is contained in sixty lines (ll. 81–140) while Lizzie's is related in a passage of twice that length (ll. 329–449). But for all the space Rossetti has expended on the second goblin experience, its meaning is unequivocal, leaving little room for dispute. As little as we may have sympathized with Lizzie earlier, her confrontation with the goblins is a selfless, courageous, and loving act impossible to discredit. Rossetti is careful to show that Lizzie's act signals a radical departure from her habitually cautious, unadventuresome posture. That her behavior is out of character makes it all the more admirable. Lizzie

> Longed to buy fruit to comfort her [Laura],
> But feared to pay too dear,
> She thought of Jeanie in her grave,
> Who should have been a bride.
> . . . .
> Till Laura dwindling
> Seemed knocking at Death's door:
> Then Lizzie weighed no more
> Better and worse;
> But put a silver penny in her purse,
> Kissed Laura, crossed the heath with clumps of furze
> At twilight, halted by the brook:
> And for the first time in her life
> Began to listen and look.
>
> (C, I: 19)

The development in Lizzie's character is one of the best results of the goblin episode; in part, this change is what makes "Goblin Market" a moral tale. For Lizzie's brave act serves as a correction of her earlier self-containment and inattention—a posture that was, in its own way, unproductive and barren. By transcending her own timidity and anxiety, Lizzie has learned a necessary and valuable lesson about her own capabilities and the virtues of self-abandonment: not the riotous, sensual variety of Laura's experience, but the generous kind required by love. What saves Lizzie from the dangers of her own attitude, Laura from imminent death, and the poem from meaninglessness is, very simply, Lizzie's love for Laura. On the narrative level alone, it is Lizzie's loving act, her need "to share" "her sister's cankerous care" (ll. 300–301), that turns what would otherwise have been a senseless tragedy into a useful, meaningful, moral story. By itself, Laura's goblin experience has been pointless, its ambiguity destructive of any coherent message; but the addition of Lizzie's act of courage founded in love turns the earlier episode into a story with a constructive, moral meaning: selfless, devoted love is a wonderful, powerful force. Significantly, this message is not presented as a parable about the dangers of particular kinds of activity. In fact, Laura's riotous experience with the goblins' fruits is not repudiated anywhere in the poem. When Laura tells her and Lizzie's children the story "of her early prime, / Those pleasant days long gone / Of not-returning time," she does not caution the children about the evil goblin men, nor, in her narrative re-creation of her past, does she seem in the least chastened by her goblin experience.[11] She

> Would talk about the haunted glen,
> The wicked, quaint fruit-merchant men,
> Their fruits like honey to the throat
> But poison in the blood;
> (Men sell not such in any town)
>   (C, I: 25)

but there is no note of self-reproach or contrition in her report. To repudiate the goblins and her experience with them would be to deny their importance, and they have been as important as the moral Lizzie creates by her confrontation of the goblins; without their presence, just as without Lizzie's act, there would be no story. Both are essential components.

From a broader angle, this is precisely the argument made in "Goblin Market" about the nature of art. Creations of the imagination can only be

---

11. Mermin, "Heroic Sisterhood in 'Goblin Market,' " 117.

called art if they are unified by, interpretable in terms of, some overarching moral principle. In this case, the moral is the principle of love, or *caritas.* Laura's rich experience with the goblins' fruit is itself fruitless without a positive meaning—a meaning the episode lacks until it is connected, in this case by dramatic means, to Lizzie's act. This fusion makes possible Laura's concluding poem. The circumstances necessary for its creation constitute Rossetti's definition of poetry: Poetry requires sensitivity, imagination, and curiosity, but those elements must be tempered by, and finally expressive of, a clear moral vision. Laura's goblin experience creates the opportunity for Lizzie's act, and Lizzie, in turn, saves Laura from barrenness and death so that she can live to create her own poetic rendering of both parts of the episode. Rossetti represents the first part of Laura's poem in paraphrase:

> Laura would call the little ones
> And tell them of her early prime,
> Those pleasant days long gone
> Of not-returning time:
> Would talk about the haunted glen,
> The wicked, quaint fruit-merchant men,
> Their fruits like honey to the throat
> But poison in the blood;
> (Men sell not such in any town:)
> Would tell them how her sister stood
> In deadly peril to do her good,
> And win the fiery antidote.
>
> (C, I: 25–26)

But the conclusion of her poem—the final interpretation, or moral—is presented as poetry:

> "For there is no friend like a sister
> In calm or stormy weather;
> To cheer one on the tedious way,
> To fetch one if one goes astray,
> To lift one if one totters down,
> To strengthen whilst one stands."
>
> (C, I: 26)

At this point in "Goblin Market," Laura has the same perspective as does the narrator, who has been able to tell the entire story because she has known the outcome all along, because she has been aware of the necessary fusion of the implications of the two goblin experiences.

Neither Laura nor the narrator repudiates the initial goblin experience; but while Laura's poem uses paraphrase to gloss over the encounter, the narrator's version preserves the goblins and the fruit feast in great detail and makes them, with all their rich and immediate gratifications, always accessible. While the goblins themselves disappear from the neighborhood, the experience they offered, though ultimately unproductive, is nonetheless constantly available, within the artifact of the poem, to the narrator and to Laura; the problem of transience has been solved through art. Indeed, the permanent availability of the initial goblin experience makes up for the undeniable fact that Laura's poem at the end of "Goblin Market" is far less exciting, less rich, and less suggestive than are the narrator's rendering of the earlier part of the poem and Laura's own description of her feast immediately following the experience (ll. 165–83). The vibrant, passionate, joyous language of that poetry has been replaced at the conclusion of the poem by language that is unmistakably unimaginative and prosaic. Clearly, the monotonous rhyme, the dreary, humdrum beat, the predictable rhythm of Laura's last lines are far removed from the colorful, delightfully unpredictable style characterizing most of "Goblin Market." Artistically, something is lost through the addition of the final moral; for Rossetti, this loss is necessary if poetry is to be an acceptable form of expression. But if we remember that the earlier parts of the poem are ineradicably part of her statement, that they are as permanently available as is the stylistically disappointing resolution, we will see the ending as far less of a capitulation. In a sense, Rossetti's creation of "Goblin Market" allows her to have it both ways. She makes the point she had to make about the necessary morality of art, and she also solves the problem of the transience and inaccessibility of intensely gratifying experience by permanently folding into the poem Laura's experience with the goblins.

Considering Rossetti's misgivings about sexual relationships with men, her attraction to the poetic vocation, and her uneasiness over the requirements of that vocation, we must see in the final situation of "Goblin

Market"—the mature lives of Laura and Lizzie—a world exactly suited to the poet's conflicting needs. In the quiet, domestic life of the two sisters and their children, Rossetti has created a female world entirely free of dependence on men. The security and excitement offered by men in earlier poems are here supplied by other sources: security, by the relationship with the provenly dependable Lizzie; excitement, by Laura's ability to recreate the goblin experience at will. There is neither deception nor entrapment in the relationship between the two sisters. Further, in this arrangement, Laura is a mother as well as a poet. Her poetic faculties, though somewhat tamed, perhaps, are still functioning, but not at the expense of motherhood. While there is evidence, both within the poems and the biography, that Rossetti did not believe herself to be suited for marriage, it is clear that the relinquishment of motherhood necessitated by her decision to remain single always pained her. In a number of poems, she expresses deep regret over being "barren in life." She was devoted to her own nieces and nephews and respected the institution of motherhood enormously.[12] In the little matriarchy at the end of "Goblin Market," Laura, the poet figure, is given what would have been for Rossetti an ideal combination: children (whose father's identity is not revealed), security, independence, and the ability to create poetry. Clearly, such an arrangement was not possible in Rossetti's own society, but one of the great virtues of poetry for Rossetti was its ability to create, if only in fantasy, what was denied in reality.

As we shall see, Christina Rossetti's poetics, as defined in "Goblin Market" and developed further in later poems, are partially a reflection of a wider aesthetic movement in Victorian England—Tractarian poetic theory. But her insistence on the morality of poetry must also be seen as the means by which she reconciled her choice of career, about which she was greatly troubled, with the social norms and expectations of her day. The morality of Rossetti's poetic theory justified and validated her intensely powerful need to write poetry. For while Rossetti's position as a single, professional woman poet was at most anomalous, the unrestrained expression and gratification of wildness, vanity, and selfishness inherent in creative activity were, for a woman, effectively prohibited. Rossetti was

12. Mackenzie Bell, *Christina Rossetti: A Biographical and Critical Study* (4th ed.; London, 1898), 111–12.

justified as a poet as long as she felt her poetry expressed moral truth. Much of Rossetti's poetry lacks a binding moral principle or single aesthetic interpretation; for much of her career, she was impelled to write poetry for other than moral reasons. But "Goblin Market" reveals the extent of the conflict born of those other reasons and marks a momentous step toward the resolution of that conflict.

FIVE

The Poetry of Discovery

or Christina Rossetti, writing poetry was a tremendously powerful act, serving as an alembic through which all that was painful or confusing could be rendered beautiful and intelligible. Rossetti was a complicated woman with diverse and often conflicting needs, and her poetry reflected this complexity; nevertheless, all her poetry was unified by this common transformative function. Through the poetic act, Rossetti could recast the unsatisfactory conditions of her temporal existence into beautiful and permanent experience. As in "A Birthday," poetry could turn the transience of mortal joy into a gorgeous artifact carved "in doves and pomegranates, / And peacocks with a hundred eyes; / . . . in gold and silver grapes, / In leaves and silver fleurs-delys." As Rossetti so brilliantly expounds in "Goblin Market," poetry could also transform through its power to unify and explain the seeming contradictions and ambiguities of experience that she found so disturbing. Rossetti's coherent, moral outlook became for her a vision both poetic and religious. Rightly practiced, writing poetry was the process that could render sense from nonsense, order from chaos, unity from ambiguity. Further, as the poems about failed love consistently demonstrate, the creation of poetry was the means through which deprivation could be transformed into restitution, pain into peace, and confusion into truth. Even the condition of being a poet wrought a reinterpretation of the circumstances of Christina Rossetti's own life, changing her singleness from a misfortune into a professional requirement; as with the heroines of her ballads, Rossetti's spinsterhood was the condition that ultimately fostered autonomy, strength, and creativity.

To transform experience was the central impetus of Rossetti's religious poetry as well as of her secular poetry. This objective unifies the entire canon, finally making any distinction between "devotional" and "general" poems a measure of degree, not kind. The frame of reference may have widened, the plane of discourse may have moved, but the issues, methods, and objectives of Rossetti's 450 religious poems are virtually identical with those of her secular poems. The religious verse, like the love poetry discussed earlier, documents the process through which dissatisfaction, confusion, and despair are reformulated into a positive, coherent condition.[1] If we see the transformations wrought by Rossetti's poetry as existing on a continuum between the temporary and mortal on the one hand, and the permanent and divine on the other, Rossetti's religious poetry would be placed near the latter end. This is the primary distinction between the secular and the religious poems.

The continuity of a poetic canon that to many appears to be fractured or, at the least, highly diverse reflects its particular historical context. Christina Rossetti's personal æsthetic—her understanding and practice of the poetic impulse—was perfectly coincident with, and unquestionably influenced by, the æsthetic principles of the Tractarian phase of the Oxford movement. (The dates of the Tractarian phase of the Oxford movement are generally agreed to be 1833, the date of John Keble's Assize Sermon, to 1845, the date of John Henry Newman's departure for Rome.) Jerome McGann and John O. Waller have argued persuasively for the need to set Rossetti's religious poetry within the context of her evangelical background, McGann going so far as to say that the Adventist doctrine of soul sleep is "the single most important enabling principle in Rossetti's religious poetry . . . [that] no other idea contributed so much to the concrete and specific character of her work."[2] As McGann points out, a substantial number of Rossetti's poems work from the premillennialist belief in the suspension, or "sleep," of souls. As a specific doctrine, soul sleep indisputably influenced Rossetti's poetic voice, though to call it the "single most important enabling principle in

1.   The composition dates of most of Rossetti's religious poetry are unknown. According to Eleanor Thomas, only 87 of the 450 religious poems were written before 1866. Thomas, *Christina Georgina Rossetti,* 191.

2.   McGann, "The Religious Poetry of Christina Rossetti," 135; John O. Waller, "Christ's Second Coming."

Rossetti's religious poetry" may be too sweeping and exclusive a claim. Still, in arguing for the necessity of placing Rossetti's poetry within a particular religious and historical context, McGann and Waller have contributed much to Rossetti scholarship. Without question, our appreciation of a good part of Christina Rossetti's poetry is enhanced by an understanding of certain specific doctrines that are unfamiliar to us. But it is at a broad, general level that this religious sensibility is most valuable as a gloss to her poetry.

Rossetti's religious background was an incongruous, but, for its time, not unusual, combination of Low Church Evangelicalism and High Church Tractarianism. Christina was raised in the former tradition by her mother and, like many of her contemporaries, was attracted in the early 1840s by the Anglo-Catholicism of Newman, E. B. Pusey, and Keble. After 1843, when the Rossetti women started attending Christ Church, Albany Street, Christina's conversion to Tractarianism was complete. While it is entirely possible that Christina Rossetti never read any of the seminal documents of the Tractarian divines, her religious beliefs were undoubtedly influenced by the general tenor of the Tractarian period; her poetry, by its central aesthetic assumptions. She did read Keble's *Christian Year* ("the volume that brought home to the age the literary practice of Tractarianism"), admired Isaac Williams' poetry, and admitted "indebtedness to Cardinal Newman."[3] Her most significant and influential contact with Tractarianism was in the sermons of the Reverend William Dodsworth, one of the central figures of the Oxford movement and Perpetual Curate of Christina's Christ Church beginning in 1837. (Soon after his resignation in 1850, Dodsworth converted to Roman Catholicism.)

Christina Rossetti recorded few comments on the various and complex theological issues of the Tractarian movement, but her poetry continually represents and affirms the aesthetic implications of Tractarian dogma. As G. B. Tennyson points out in his study of Tractarian poetic theory, the Oxford movement was as much an aesthetic reorientation as it was a strictly theological one. In Rossetti's case, the aesthetic implications of the movement had a far greater and longer-lived influence than did its theological subtleties. Whether or not she was aware that a "self-consistent

---

and coherent aesthetic theory" could be drawn from the major Tractarian documents, her poetry testifies to her absorption in, and practice of, such a theory.[4]

For Rossetti and the Tractarian theologians writing in the nineteenth century, the universe was ordered, intelligible, and moral; the enabling force behind such a universe was a just, benevolent God. The world's evil and confusion were only illusory, functions of an incomplete understanding or a misinterpretation of the meaning of God's creation. Rightly construed, all natural phenomena were symbols of God and religious truth, God's way of gradually leading men and women to an apprehension of His truth. As Newman wrote in his autobiography, "Material phenomena are both the types and the instruments of real things unseen." This belief in the divine organization and significance of all things, which the Tractarians referred to as *Analogy*, was by no means a nineteenth-century innovation; it can be traced back to the early church fathers—to Saint Paul, Saint Irenaeus, Saint Basil, and Saint Ambrose. In his explanation of Analogy in *Tract 89* (1840), Keble cites the Pauline text "The invisible things of Him are understood by the things which are made."[5] But Tractarian writers such as Keble, Newman, and Isaac Williams did more than revive what the Fathers called "mysticism"; they used Analogy as a central foundation of an aesthetic theory that was as far-reaching as was any theological contribution made by the Tractarian movement.[6]

The other critical Tractarian principle to have extensive aesthetic influence was the doctrine of *Reserve*. G. B. Tennyson gives the following definition:

The idea of Reserve is that since God is ultimately incomprehensible, we can know Him only indirectly; His truth is hidden and given to us only in a manner suited to our capacities for apprehending it. Moreover, it is both unnecessary and undesirable that God and religious truth generally should be disclosed in their fullness at once to all regardless of the differing capacities of individuals to apprehend such things. God Himself in His economy has only gradually in time revealed such things as we know about Him. Both the sacredness and the complexity of the subject of religious truth are such that they require a holding back

4. Tennyson, *Victorian Devotional Poetry,* 10, 13.

5. John Henry Newman, *Apologia pro vita sua,* ed. Martin Svaglic (Oxford, 1967), 29; John Keble, *Tract 89,* in *Tracts for the Times* (London, 1840), 152.

6. Tennyson, *Victorian Devotional Poetry,* 10.

and a gradual revelation as the disposition and understanding of the recipient mature.

For the Tractarians, Reserve characterized not only God's gradual way of revealing truth but also, ideally, the poet's style of disclosing God's truth. Analogy and Reserve are closely connected; as Tennyson puts it, "Analogy is God's way of practicing Reserve."[7]

As Keble and others made explicit, the doctrine of Analogy had unmistakable aesthetic implications. The practice of searching for God's truth in His carefully laid-out universe, of finding meaning in material reality and moral lessons in all experience, was, for the Tractarians and Christina Rossetti, both a religious and a poetic activity. According to Keble, the "Poetical," "Moral," and "Mystical" (or "Theological") approaches to the world were different degrees of this universal drive to ascribe meaning to experience, a meaning that is allowed, or set in place, by God. Keble wrote, in *Tract 89,*

Of these, the Poetical comes first in order, as the natural groundwork or rudiment of the two. This is indicated by all languages, and by the conversation of uneducated persons in all countries. There is every where a tendency to make the things we see represent the things we do not see, to invent or remark mutual associations between them, to call the one sort by the names of the other.

The second, the Moral use of the material world, is the improvement of the poetical or imaginative use of it, for the good of human life and conduct, by considerate persons, according to the best of their own judgment, antecedent to, or apart from all revealed information on the subject.

In like manner, the Mystical, or Christian, or Theological use of it is the reducing to a particular set of symbols and associations, which we have reason to believe has, more or less, the authority of the GREAT CREATOR Himself.

Elsewhere, Keble wrote that the exercise of the poetic faculty, the poet's recognition of the

various images and similes of things, and all other poetic charms, are not merely the play of a keen and clever mind, nor to be put down as empty fancies: but rather they guide us by gentle hints and no uncertain signs, to the very utterances of Nature, or we may more truly say, of the Author of Nature.

As long as it is informed by a belief in God's divine plan, the creation of poetry, with its symbolization and its suggestion of correspondences, is a

7. *Ibid.,* 45, 47.

form of religious experience leading poet and reader alike to a fuller understanding of a divine and moral universe. For the Tractarians, poetry and prayer are indistinguishable, each a sign of cherishing "the vision of something more beautiful, greater and more lovable, than all the mortal eye can see."[8]

Christina Rossetti's poetry—both religious and secular—is based on, and represents the Tractarian belief in, a symbolic world created and presided over by a loving God. The transforming properties of Rossetti's poetry are firmly set within this understanding of the universe and of the role of poetry. Rossetti's constant urge to recreate, to reformulate, and to resolve is justified or allowed by the unity, order, and benevolence of God's creation. For Rossetti, such miracles can only be worked within a coherent, self-consistent moral system, the capstone of which is God's powerful love. Her belief in the existence of multiple analogues of God's love, of many parallel planes of this truth, is an important backdrop to our appreciation of her poetry: This faith explains her parabolic poetic method, enables the reformulating imperative of her poetry, and justifies her choice of the poetic vocation.

Christina Rossetti's poetic method reveals the correspondence between seemingly unconnected planes of experience—specifically, between the material and the moral. Because of her belief in a thoroughly moral universe, Rossetti, unlike many of her contemporaries, was able to view its symbolic arrangement with comparative equanimity. Her insistence on a fairly narrow range of meaning distinguishes her from other nineteenth-century writers—from Dante Gabriel Rossetti, for example, who in "The Woodspurge" finds relief from the *lack* of natural symbolism; and from Melville, who explores the countless significations of symbols. Christina Rossetti is not content to remain ambivalent toward symbols, as Keats's speakers are toward the nightingale or the Grecian urn. The firmness of Rossetti's religious conviction gives her symbols a semantic and emotional stability that more skeptical or religiously troubled writers either did not want or could not have. Given the perfectly wrought plan under which the universe operated, the phenomenon of one thing signifying another was, for Rossetti, not disruptive and threatening but sensible and comfort-

8. Keble, *Tract 89*, p. 143; John Keble, *Lectures on Poetry*, trans. E. K. Francis (Oxford, 1912), II, 481, 482–83.

ing. While the exact correspondence between the material world and its spiritual significance might be difficult to identify, the connection existed, Rossetti was confident, and it was morally instructive and coherent. As she wrote in "'Consider the Lilies of the Field'" (1853),

> The merest grass
> Along the roadside where we pass,
> Lichen and moss and sturdy weed,
> Tell of His love who sends the dew,
> The rain and sunshine too,
> To nourish one small seed.
>
> (C, II: 76)

One of the clearest statements of Rossetti's belief in the symbolic, or analogical, arrangement of a divinely ordered, beneficent universe is the second part of the poem "They shall be as white as snow" (date of composition unknown; first appearance in *Verses* of 1893):

> Thy lilies drink the dew,
> Thy lambs the rill, and I will drink them too;
> For those in purity
> And innocence are types, dear Lord, of Thee.
> The fragrant lily flower
> Bows and fulfils Thy Will its lifelong hour;
> The lamb at rest and play
> Fulfils Thy Will in gladness all the day;
> They leave tomorrow's cares
> Until the morrow, what it brings it bears.
> And I, Lord, would be such;
> Not high or great or anxious overmuch,
> But pure and temperate,
> Earnest to do Thy Will betimes and late,
> Fragrant with love and praise
> And innocence thro' all my appointed days;
> Thy lily I would be,
> Spotless and sweet, Thy lamb to follow Thee.[9]
>
> (C, II: 256)

9. R. W. Crump (ed.), *The Complete Poems of Christina Rossetti,* II, 14. Rossetti's final volume of poetry, *Verses* (London, 1893), contains poems drawn primarily from three earlier books of prose and poetry: *Called to be Saints: The Minor Festivals*

The speakers of Rossetti's religious poems are not always so clearly aware of this correspondence between natural phenomena and spiritual truth, or of their ultimate place within that order. Desperate and confused at the outset, the speakers literally talk themselves into hope and understanding. In many cases, this process of enlightenment is represented by the speaker's gradual recognition of the moral significance of material phenomena, or of the spiritual implications of experience.

Confident in the spiritual significance of material reality, Rossetti often used a parabolic method, presenting material phenomena as a basis for spiritual instruction. Her parabolic approach maintains a correspondence (which implies a separation, a distance) between the signifier and the signified, whereas some of the poets of her time (Hopkins is an obvious example) tend to collapse the signified into the signifier. In Hopkins' poetry, the reader's sense of the spiritual, the noumenal, is controlled by the nature of the images employed. Rossetti does not write allegory in the sense that her images become stick figures to illustrate abstract qualities, but she retains a gap between what is said and what is meant, as do parables. And, as in most parables, what is said becomes an exemplum for a system of belief having its basis outside the work of art.

Poems using the natural world to symbolize spiritual truth are legion in the Rossetti canon and span her entire career. A simple example is "God's Acre," which first appeared in *Verses*. The relationship between unsprouted seeds and the spring sun is implicitly analogous to the relationship between humanity and God.

> Hail, garden of confident hope!
>> Where sweet seeds are quickening in darkness and cold;
>>> For how sweet and how young will they be
>> When they pierce thro' the mould.
> Balm, myrtle, and heliotrope
>> There watch and there wait out of sight for their Sun:
>>> While the Sun, which they see not, doth see
>> Each and all one by one.
>>>>> (C, II: 319)

Devotionally Studied (1881); *Time Flies: A Reading Diary* (1885); and *The Face of the Deep: A Devotional Commentary on the Apocalypse* (1892).

Based upon Rossetti's conviction of the congruence between material and spiritual reality, this nature poem is a lesson in the need for patience and in the certainty of God's devotion. In a similar vein is "'Who hath despised the day of small things?'" (also in *Verses*):

> As violets so be I recluse and sweet,
>> Cheerful as daisies unaccounted rare,
> Still sunward-gazing from a lowly seat,
>> Still sweetening wintry air.
>
> While half-awakened Spring lags incomplete,
>> While lofty forest trees tower bleak and bare,
> Daisies and violets own remotest heat
>> And bloom and make them fair.
>
> (C, II: 257)

The lesson of this poem is also made possible by the unstated assumption that God's creations—his violets and daisies—are signs of truth, examples of right conduct.

The 1849 poem "Symbols," which first appeared as part of Rossetti's story *Maude: Prose and Verse* (1850), contains a dramatic enactment of this parabolic method. In the first three stanzas, the speaker describes the disappointment of her hopes for natural renewal:

> I watched a rosebud very long
>> Brought on by dew and sun and shower,
>> Waiting to see the perfect flower:
> Then, when I thought it should be strong,
>> It opened at the matin hour
>> And fell at evensong.
>
> I watched a nest from day to day,
>> A green nest full of pleasant shade,
>> Wherein three speckled eggs were laid:
> But when they should have hatched in May,
>> The two old birds had grown afraid
>> Or tired, and flew away.
>
> Then in my wrath I broke the bough
>> That I had tended so with care,
>> Hoping its scent should fill the air;
> I crushed the eggs, not heeding how

Their ancient promise had been fair:
I would have vengeance now.

(C, I: 75)

In the final stanza, the speaker is made to understand the correspondence
between these two natural failures and her own barrenness as well as the
lack of correspondence between her impatience and God's tolerance:

But the dead branch spoke from the sod,
And the eggs answered me again:
Because we failed dost thou complain?
Is thy wrath just? And what if God,
Who waiteth for thy fruits in vain,
Should also take the rod?

(C, I: 75–76)

The events of the poem serve as a parable about God's love and the
speaker's unworthiness to receive that love. The frailty of the rose and the
barrenness of the eggs reflect the speaker's own weaknesses. While the
speaker cannot tolerate these failures, she is reminded that God does
tolerate such shortcomings in her. She is the one element out of joint in
this analogy, and the disjunction is doubly instructive: it is a lesson in
humility and in the magnitude of God's love. What makes this parable
possible is the poet's belief in an internally consistent, morally coherent
universe where all experience has spiritual significance. As Rossetti's
poetic method matures she will no longer rely on revelation through
talking branches and crushed eggs, but will make discoveries through the
speaking of the poem.

The analogical relationship between the visible and the invisible is also
the foundation that allows the speaker of "Symbols" to translate an initial
situation of failure and loss into one of gain and understanding as do the
speakers of the love poems and the later poems discussed in this chapter.
What the speaker initially assumed to be a useless tale of frailty and
destruction is decoded into a narrative of spiritual instruction. What
enables the decoding or translation is the beneficent congruence between
different planes of experience. If "the invisible things of Him are understood by the things which are made," as Keble's *Tract 89* quotes Saint Paul,
then all experience, all material signs, however senseless they may appear,
can yield some good. In "Symbols," a correct interpretation of natural

phenomena (the fate of the rosebud and the eggs), based upon a recognition of the symbolic nature of God's universe, discovers positive truth in seeming failure.

We have seen already that for Rossetti the ability to read symbols correctly is crucial. In "Amor Mundi," Rossetti suggests that the young woman's descent into Hell could have been prevented if she had stopped to interpret the ambiguous portent of the meteor. And in "Goblin Market," Laura almost dies from her indulgence in the chaotic, uninterpreted stuff of the imagination. It is only the addition of Lizzie's brave act, which serves as a unifying moral, or interpretation, that turns the goblin experience to some good. Although Rossetti's Tractarian world view is not at all explicit in these two poems, this perspective or something like it does inform her use of symbol. Both poems operate from an unstated conviction of an ordered, moral universe where material reality has discernible and unified moral significance.

This conviction enabled not only Christina Rossetti's parabolic poetic method but also the central transformative impulse of her poetry. As we saw in "Goblin Market," one facet of this imperative is the need to explain the often-crippling ambiguities of experience. Rossetti's belief in an overarching divine order was the source of her ability to disarm and unify bewildering contradictions. Her faith does not so much *resolve* ambiguity and paradox, which suggests a dialectical process almost entirely absent from her work, as it undermines them or erases them, finally revealing that uncertainty is only in the eye of the beholder. In short, those who are beleaguered by ambiguity suffer from an incomplete vision that can be cleared by faith. Even Rossetti's least-religious poems incline toward a faith in the ultimate explicability and unity of experience; they assume the existence of a single truth. "Goblin Market" is an extended example of Rossetti's insistence on the final unification of ambiguity. She does not deny its existence; nor does she even attempt to explain ambiguity. She does, however, literally subordinate it to the final moral of the tale. In the narrative, the ambiguity of the goblins is only useful as a way of enabling the revelation of the poem's ultimate message about love. Dramatically speaking, ambiguity is cast in a supporting, not a principal, role.

In the later poems, Rossetti's inclination toward a single truth capable of dismantling all contradiction is expressed in strictly religious terms, but it is the same tendency we have seen throughout her work. Late in her career, the paradox most frequently at issue is the traditionally troubling incongruity of God's great love for a frail and undeserving humanity, of the simultaneous distance and proximity of God. In the first sonnet of two under the title "Cried out with Tears," the speaker begins by lamenting her inadequacy and unworthiness.

> Lord, I believe, help Thou mine unbelief:
>   Lord, I repent, help mine impenitence:
>   Hide not Thy Face from me, nor spurn me hence,
> Nor utterly despise me in my grief;
> Nor say me nay, who worship with the thief
>   Bemoaning my so long lost innocence:—
> Ah me! my penitence a fresh offence,
> Too tardy and too tepid and too brief.
>
>   (C, II: 184–85)

The paradoxes in the first two lines (the first taken directly from Mark 9:24) are rich: First, and most obviously, they reveal the speaker's broken condition, her habit of believing and doubting at the same time, of repenting and refusing to repent. Like "the undeciphered, solemn signal of help or hurt" in "Amor Mundi," the speaker's position is fraught with contradictory possibilities. Implicit as well within the opening of the sonnet is the psychological fact that believing is never as certain as knowing, that belief always carries with it a leap of faith and thus an edge of unbelief. The paradoxes also introduce the central problem of the poem: the vast difference and distance between God and the speaker. These two lines suggest the speaker's awareness that her belief and repentance, though sincere, seem paltry in the face of God's expectations—hence her prayer for help: "help Thou mine unbelief . . . help mine impenitence." In the rest of the octave, the speaker's prayer that her unworthiness be ignored ("Hide not Thy Face from me, nor spurn me hence, / Nor utterly despise me in my grief") actually develops the assumption of her unworthiness.

In the sestet, the distance and difference between the speaker and God are starkly rendered in terms of their respective physical positions.

> Lord, must I perish, I who look to Thee?
>   Look Thou upon me, bid me live, not die;
>   Say, "Come," say not "Depart," tho' Thou art just:

> Yea, Lord, be mindful how out of the dust
> I look to Thee while Thou dost look on me,
> Thou Face to face with me and Eye to eye.
>
> (C, II: 185)

Although the sestet begins by suggesting the vast distance between God and the speaker, we realize that the speaker's prayer, her act of speaking this poem, gradually changes her perception of that distance by the final two lines of the sonnet. In the thirteenth line, she describes the simultaneous difference and identity between herself and God. Their activities are significantly different, though only a preposition keeps them from being identical ("I look *to* Thee while Thou dost look *on* me" [my emphasis]), but the similarity of the language and syntax suggests a possible union. In the fourteenth line, that possibility is even more pronounced; now only a capitalization, albeit a tremendously significant one, distinguishes them: "Thou Face to face with me and Eye to eye." The conclusion of the poem reminds us of the difference between God and the speaker and demonstrates how much distance has been bridged through the speaking of this poem. The outright contradictions of the first two lines ("I believe, help Thou mine unbelief") have been replaced by virtual identification ("Thou Face to face with me and Eye to eye"). The final line paradoxically suggests simultaneous intimacy and distance, but it also indicates how much closer the speaker has come to God through her prayer. Throughout the poem, the speaker's fear has been that God would not look upon her; but by the final line, she has the confidence to present herself and God in a position of intense and mutual observation.

Although the speaker has gained much in the course of this first sonnet, its final suggestion of identity, difference, and confrontation is fraught with tension. The succeeding sonnet continues the movement toward union between God and the speaker, finally dissolving the tension that permeated the first sonnet. Although the second poem appears to begin in the same paradoxical vein as did the first, we become quickly aware that the speaker's attitude has changed. Self-critical and fearful in the first sonnet, she is now confident of God's love, asking him not just to notice her but to strengthen the union between them. Clearly, the movement represented in the first sonnet has fortified the speaker's faith in God's love. After reminding us in line 1 of the paradoxical tone of the first sonnet and of its central conceit of *looking,* the speaker moves away from confusion and uncertainty.

> O Lord, on Whom we gaze and dare not gaze,
>   Increase our faith that gazing we may see,
>   And seeing love, and loving worship Thee
> Thro' all our days, our long and lengthening days.
> O Lord, accessible to prayer and praise,
>   Kind Lord, Companion of the two or three,
>   Good Lord, be gracious to all men and me,
> Lighten our darkness and amend our ways.
> Call up our hearts to Thee, that where Thou art
>   Our treasure and our heart may dwell at one:
>   Then let the pallid moon pursue her sun,
> So long as it shall please Thee, far apart,—
>   Yet art Thou with us, Thou to Whom we run,
> We hand in hand with Thee and heart in heart.
>
>   (C, II: 185)

It is as if the direct contemplation of God in the first sonnet, with its suggestion of union or identity, has completely changed the speaker's vision of God. God is no longer spurning and despising but is "accessible to prayer and praise," a "Kind Lord," a "Good Lord." The speaker is preoccupied, not with contradiction and deprivation, but with increase and union. The thirteenth line reintroduces the paradoxical note—"Yet art Thou with us, Thou to Whom we run"—but the poem as a whole has given us the key for explaining the contradiction. God's love, of which the speaker has been confident throughout the poem, is the key—the single, ultimate truth that makes sense out of apparent contradiction, that offers a heavenly union capable of wiping out all difference and distance. The final line of the second sonnet, "We hand in hand with Thee and heart in heart," echoes the final line of the first, "Thou Face to face with me and Eye to eye," but makes the union more complete and more intimate. At the end of the second sonnet, which seems to refer to the speaker's union with God after death, not even a capitalization distinguishes God and the speaker.

These linked sonnets make much the same point as did "Goblin Market," though on a different plane: Preoccupation with ambiguity and contradiction is a temporary developmental phase meaningless in itself but necessary for the final perception or enactment of love, the gift that makes sense out of confusion and brings light from darkness, hope from despair. We see this pattern (less skillfully wrought) in poems written before "Goblin Market." In "The Heart Knoweth Its Own Bitterness" (1857), the speaker controlled her frustration with the disparities, distances, and contradictions of mortal life by looking to her ultimate union with a loving Christ: "I full of Christ and Christ of me." And, similarly, in "The Lowest Room" (1856), the promise of Heaven helped the elder sister tolerate the disparity between what she wanted and what she received:

> Yea, sometimes still I lift my heart
> To the Archangelic trumpet-burst,
> When all deep secrets shall be shown,
> And many last be first.

Rossetti's faith in divine order and love makes possible another repeated achievement in her poetry: the speaker's movement from despair and confusion to faith and understanding. We saw this development unfold in the "Cried out with Tears" sonnets, in which the act of speaking the poem brought the speaker progressively closer to an apprehension of God's love and of her own worthiness. For Rossetti, poetry is ideally a process of discovery that leads the speaker or poet unerringly to a recognition of truth—of the final harmony of all things and of her secure place in that harmonious system. In this sense, poetry and prayer are virtually synonymous; indeed, the majority of Rossetti's "devotional" poems would fit Keble's definition of prayer as a way of "seek[ing] the Deity."[10] Although Rossetti's secular poems are not involved in a search for God, a great number of them exhibit this same process of change and self-discovery on the speaker's part. The poems discussed at the end of Chapter Three offer some of the best examples of this transformative function of poetry. In "Cousin Kate," "Brandons Both," and " 'The Iniquity of the Fathers Upon the Children,' " three women discover strength, self-sufficiency, and identity in being single. The process of telling their stories (the poems themselves) turns them from rejected, miserable women into independent, self-reliant, self-respecting heroines. Rossetti's practice of representing such transforming self-discoveries is founded upon a faith distinctly

---

10. Keble, *Lectures on Poetry,* II, 482.

similar to that which informs the religious poems. Rossetti could not have written lines such as these (from " 'The Iniquity' ") without tremendous faith in herself—or, more generally, in the power and worth of the individual:

> I'll not blot out my shame
> With any man's good name;
> But nameless as I stand,
> My hand is my own hand,
> And nameless as I came
> I go to the dark land.
>
> (C, I: 178)

The confidence and self-love discovered by the speakers of the ballads and other love poems are a partial version of a broader belief in a divinely ordered universe of which each individual is a precious part. It is this wider faith, of course, that informs the devotional poems, but it is also implicit in the secular poems. Without this belief, self-discoveries such as we see in "Cousin Kate" and "Brandons Both" could not occur. In both the secular and the devotional poems, the key that reveals to the speaker that truth about herself is the creation of poetry—a process that discloses correspondences and seeks out harmonies.

One of the finest examples of self-transformation based on divine order and achieved through poetry is the early religious poem "A Better Resurrection" (1857). A poem about the painful process of rediscovering faith, it is also as deft and rich a testament to the regenerative properties of poetry as Rossetti ever wrote. Like so much of Rossetti's poetry, "A Better Resurrection" begins in despair and stasis (much like the condition in the sonnet "Cobwebs"):

> I have no wit, no words, no tears;
>   My heart within me like a stone
> Is numbed too much for hopes or fears;
>   Look right, look left, I dwell alone;
> I lift mine eyes, but dimmed with grief
>   No everlasting hills I see;
> My life is in the falling leaf:
>   O Jesus, quicken me.
>
> (C, I: 68)

The speaker's speechlessness ("I have no wit, no words") is a measure of her deep despair, of her inability to see the harmony of things, her place in the universe, and her relationship to God. That the language of this first stanza is comparatively free of poetic tropes emphasizes the speaker's spiritual sterility; she can make no connections. Emotionally and physically numb, she prays desperately to a distant Christ for revival: "O Jesus, quicken me."

In the second stanza, the speaker begins to talk herself into some hope. Picking up one of the few figures of speech from stanza 1 ("My life is in the falling leaf"), she develops the analogy between her spiritual condition and nature's yearly cycle.

> My life is like a faded leaf,
>   My harvest dwindled to a husk;
> Truly my life is void and brief
>   And tedious in the barren dusk;
> My life is like a frozen thing,
>   No bud nor greenness can I see:
> Yet rise it shall—the sap of Spring;
>   O Jesus, rise in me.
>   (C, I: 68)

The act of discovering correspondences proves to be self-generating, as one figure leads to another. The more connections the speaker sees, the closer she is to realizing, as she does in lines 15 and 16, that her situation is not hopeless. Like the "faded leaf," the "harvest dwindled," and the "frozen thing," she too will revive: "Yet rise it shall—the sap of Spring." The process of discovering analogies, which has come naturally out of the speaker's desire to express herself, leads her to a recognition of her place in God's order and of her increasing proximity to Christ. By the end of the second stanza, she has realized or remembered that she is not alone, that Christ dwells within her ("O Jesus, rise in me").

In the third stanza, the analogizing impulse continues, but as we saw in "A Birthday," it moves away from the context of nature.

> My life is like a broken bowl,
>   A broken bowl that cannot hold
> One drop of water for my soul

Or cordial in the searching cold;
Cast in the fire the perished thing,
Melt and remould it, till it be
A royal cup for Him my King:
O Jesus, drink of me.

(C, I: 68)

Wary, perhaps, of the cyclical quality of natural renewal, wanting something more permanent and tangible to offer Christ, the speaker compares herself to a bowl, a bowl that is initially broken but that through the agency of prayer (or poetry) can be transformed into "A royal cup for Him my King." Not only is the speaker creating the artifact that is the poem, she herself is becoming something beautiful and useful and restorative. As the title of the poem suggests, she, like Christ before her, has been resurrected. And it is the analogical poetic activity, this process of discovering correspondences between herself, the world, and Christ, that has put this resurrection into operation, that has recast her mute despair into a precious offering for Christ: "A royal cup for Him my King: / O Jesus, drink of me." In "A Better Resurrection," as in so many other Rossetti poems, the act of speaking poetry regenerates, transforms, and unifies. The speaking of the poem has "made up" the speaker—given her new possibilities, new confidence, and a new identity. So close is the discovered correspondence between herself and Christ that she becomes the sacrament for Him. The speaker's achievement of wholeness and of union with Christ is echoed by the substitution in lines 22 and 23 of strong metaphor for simile; she is praying, not that her life be like a royal cup, but that it "be / A royal cup." The dropping of the "like" stands for the final bridging of all distance.

In "A Better Resurrection," as in so many of the failed-love poems, an apparent miracle has been worked for the speaker: from muteness and uselessness has come positive gain. This magic works because the speaker (and all mankind) is a precious part of a just and perfectly organized divine system. The speaking of the poem does not so much spin gold from straw as it clears the benighted vision of the speaker, who at the beginning of the poem was insensible to her part in the divine order. She and the speakers of a substantial number of the religious poems experience a gradual revelation of truth, a revelation that includes recognition of their own pricelessness, of their part in God's harmonious universe, of their promised proximity to God. These eternal truths make possible the transformations in the speakers of the religious poems; the poetic process puts these transformations into motion.

Poetry derives its great transforming power from its close affinity with prayer. In its discovery of correspondences, its seeking of God, and its revelation of truth, Rossetti's religious poetry *is* prayer, the one activity that will put the individual back in contact with God's truth. Rossetti says, in "When my heart is vexed I will complain" (date unknown), that prayer will avail, even at the day of judgment:

> "But Christ can give thee heart Who loveth thee:
> Can set thee in the eternal ecstasy
> Of His great jubilee:
> Can give thee dancing heart and shining face,
> And lips filled full of grace,
> And pleasures as the rivers and the sea.
> Who knocketh at His door
> He welcomes evermore:
> Kneel down before
> That ever-open door
> (The time is short) and smite
> Thy breast, and pray with all thy might.
> . . . .
> Tho' one but say 'Thy Will be done,'
> He hath not lost his day
> At set of sun."
>
> (C, II: 303–304)

For Rossetti, the final revealer of truth was not the poet but God— himself a divine poet whose poem was Heaven and Earth and whose tropes were nature and humanity. It is God's love and grace that work the transformation and put men and women back in harmony with the divine order, God's love that allows the exchange of "bliss for bane," "innocence for guilt, and for my stain / Whiteness most white" ("They shall be as white as snow," from *Verses*). Even in the poems that *begin* with a representation of this truth, the speakers usually undergo some learning or discovery process. In the second part of "'When I was in trouble I called upon the Lord,'" for example, the speaker begins her prayer with a recognition of God's grace and of her ideal place in his universe. But despite her initial understanding of the harmony of the universe and of her place within it, the act of praying (poem making) leads her to an enriched understanding of the truth.

> Grant us such grace that we may work Thy Will
>   And speak Thy words and walk before Thy Face,
> Profound and calm, like waters deep and still:
>   Grant us such grace.
>
>   Not hastening and not loitering in our pace
> For gloomiest valley or for sultriest hill,
>   Content and fearless on our downward race.
>
> As rivers seek a sea they cannot fill
>   But are themselves filled full in its embrace,
> Absorbed, at rest, each river and each rill:
>   Grant us such grace.
>
> (C, II: 257)

By the third stanza, the speaker's initial, simple analogy between her desired behavior and "waters deep and still" (l. 3) has developed into an extended simile of four lines, suggesting the speaker's more complete appreciation of the universe and her place in it. As she prays she discovers the profundity of the correspondence between the world, herself, and God. In short, her poem or prayer has moved her to a deeper understanding of God.

The Tractarian world view, with its belief in a system of natural and spiritual correspondences set in place by the divine symbol-maker, God, put tremendous value on the poetic faculty. Inheriting the Romantic view of the poet as visionary, the Tractarians went a step further, believing that the creation of poetry was a religious activity analogous to the work of God. Just as God shows forth his truth through his creations, so the poet reveals God through her poetry. Christina Rossetti's religious poetry unquestionably reflects this understanding of the poet's function. Whether it concentrates on the significance of a particular holy day, represents the perfection of Heaven, or is used as a prayer for grace, Rossetti's religious poetry is unified by this belief in the dynamic and sacred nature of poetry, by the conviction that poetry (and therefore the poet) reveals truth. Rossetti's verse exemplifies the Tractarian belief in the revelatory function of poetry more successfully than does the work of any of the acknowledged Tractarian poets (Isaac Williams, John Keble, and John Henry Newman, for example). Unquestionably, she deserves recognition for more than merely absorbing and practicing a particular aesthetic; in fact, the skill with which she developed this view had no parallel among her contemporaries. To compare her poetry with that of Williams, who is probably the best of the acknowledged Tractarian poets, is to realize that Rossetti was as much a leader as she was a representative.

The purpose of this chapter is not, however, to evaluate Rossetti's practice of a particular aesthetic, but to demonstrate the suitability of that aesthetic to her particular circumstances. What suited Rossetti about the Tractarian philosophy was its justification of her choice of the poetic vocation. As we have seen, the writing of poetry served a number of different and sometimes conflicting needs for Rossetti. Excusing her from the traditional female lot of mute dependence, poetry enabled her to cultivate an individual and independent voice, to recreate experience in a more satisfying form, to explore the reaches of her imagination, to mine gain and creation from the depths of despair and loss. But for all the satisfactions that writing poetry afforded Christina Rossetti, it also exacted a significant cost in the female tender of guilt—guilt for exploring her imagination, for being different, for being self-preoccupied. If her vocation had a moral or religious purpose (the Tractarian view of the poet's role), much of this guilt could be put to rest. The conflicting demands of Rossetti's asceticism and creativity, her traditionalism and nonconformity, could be satisfied by writing a certain kind of poetry, a poetry dedicated to the revelation of morality, order, and divine truth. From the earliest poems, in which the curative, restorative properties of language are revealed—poems like "Heart's Chill Between" and "An End"—to the moral-bearing "Goblin Market" to the explicitly religious poetry, Rossetti's writing was founded on the assumption that poetry must do some good. In the earlier poems, the "good" achieved by poetry was emotional and personal—the raising of the poet's own flagging spirits. But by the time she wrote "Goblin Market," Rossetti had determined that to be justifiable, her poetry must serve a larger moral end. As early as 1854, five years before the composition of "Goblin Market," Rossetti made her belief in the morality of her vocation explicit. In a letter to William

Edmonston Aytoun, she wrote, "Poetry is with me, not a mechanism, but an impulse and a reality; and . . . I know my aims in writing to be pure, and directed to that which is true and right."[11] In the final third of her career, this moral imperative widened to include a spiritual, or religious, obligation, in much the same way that Keble's classification of the moral use of the world was subsumed by the "Mystical, or Christian, or Theological use of it."[12] In the last years of her life, Rossetti's creative imagination coincided with her religious vision. Virtually all she wrote, including a number of prose works in the 1880s, originated in, and reflected a sensibility completely suffused with, traditional Christian faith. The doubt and despair that had motivated and enriched much of the earlier religious poetry almost disappeared in the final years, giving place to expressions of faith, praise, and thanksgiving. This late work does not often document the *discovery* of spiritual truth but is unwaveringly dedicated to its representation.

To twentieth-century readers, Rossetti's emphasis on "single" truths in her poetry, her discomfort with tension, ambiguity, and doubt, can seem reductive and limited. But her search for an instrument with which she could strike through the confusion of uncertainty and faithlessness was common to the age. The often-personal quality of Rossetti's poetry, its apparent inattention to the central Victorian issues directly treated by such writers as Arnold, Tennyson, and Eliot, can obscure its important affinities with the major Victorian canon. Christina Rossetti, like so many of her contemporaries, was struggling for certainty in a world seemingly determined to subvert all traditional doctrines, to undermine all accepted truths. Like Arnold and Tennyson, she sought a system of belief that could restore equilibrium, that could warrant a stabilizing faith. The faith and security she found in Anglo-Catholicism, others found in less traditional belief systems—Arnold in culture, Carlyle in work, Hardy in a stoic humanism. But she came to her particular faith only after great trial and exploration. Her discoveries of moral and spiritual truth—her poetic affirmations of a traditional Christian cosmos—were victories that she had to win again and again, in poem after poem, not complacent expressions of untried Victorian piety.

11. Harrison, "Christina Rossetti: The Poetic Vocation," 1.
12. Keble, *Tract 89*, p. 143.

Rossetti's poetry consistently gives the impression of a dynamic process of discovery and revelation; few poems in the canon read as packaged reenactments of achieved solutions. Unlike the speaker in Donne's "The Compasse," Rossetti's speakers never end where they begin; they *always* gain something through the act of speaking. Although Rossetti was a scrupulous reviser of her work, she rarely changed the central movement of a poem once it had been set down. To *write* was to discover a solution to the problem, an anodyne for the pain, a faith for the uncertainty; once that discovery was made, the poem had achieved its most compelling purpose. The ultimate source of Rossetti's faith was Christianity, but like so many of her nineteenth-century contemporaries, she also recognized the tremendous power of poetry as a revealer of truth; in her best poems, we witness this process at work.

In fact, Rossetti's poetry reveals far more than conventional Christian verities; many of her most important poems discover truths that were, for their time, socially subversive—truths about the dangers of marriage and dependence (as in "Moonshine," "The Lowest Room," and "Remember"), about the appeal of knowledge, sexuality, autonomy, and power (as in "Amor Mundi," "The Heart Knoweth Its Own Bitterness," and " 'The Iniquity of the Fathers Upon the Children' "). In these works and others, Rossetti resorts to the same technique as her American contemporary Emily Dickinson: "Tell all the truth but tell it slant." In a poem like "Remember," startling truths are hidden behind a traditional mask of female passivity—truths about male dominance, woman's resentment of this dominance, and a social system that makes an assertion of female independence more unthinkable than death. As she matured, Rossetti grew more candid in her social commentary, revealing directly in such poems as "Brandons Both" and " 'The Iniquity' " the power and self-sufficiency of her female heroines. Whether presented obliquely or directly, such observations reveal the ongoing conflict between Rossetti's sense of herself—her capabilities, inclinations, and aspirations—and the roles that were available to her.

It was in her investigation of this conflict that Rossetti found a place for herself, in her impulse to tell the truth that she discovered the role of poet. The quality of Rossetti's poetic voice—its sobriety, reserve, and clarity—disguised its social vision, a vision in which men were dispensable, women powerful and self-sufficient. Even as a doctrinally conventional and conservative religious poet, Rossetti held a position that was still socially anomalous. The preponderance of religious poems in her canon, as well as her unassuming poetic voice, obscures the implications of her choice of vocation. Had Rossetti written nothing but paeans to middle-class Victorian domesticity, her position as an independent, professional woman poet would still be remarkable. But Christina Rossetti was far from an automatic supporter of the status quo; she was a professional woman poet whose dedication to the truth led her to points of view that were as frequently unconventional as they were conformist. In her commitment to a role so contradictory to the established order and her devotion to the revelation of truth through this role, Christina Rossetti was inarguably extraordinary. Osbert Burdett maintained that the Church of England "placed its soul in peril for neglecting" Christina Rossetti.[13] It is not extravagant to direct a similar caution to students of English literature: Certainly, to ignore Christina Rossetti is to ignore a unique and compelling voice of the Victorian age.

13. Osbert Burdett, *The Beardsley Period: An Essay in Perspective* (New York, 1925), 131.

Bibliography

Abram, M. H., ed. *Norton Anthology of English Literature.* New York, 1962. 2nd ed., 1968; 3rd ed., 1974; 4th ed., 1979; 5th ed., 1986.

Battiscombe, Georgina. *Christina Rossetti: A Divided Life.* London, 1981.

Bell, Mackenzie. *Christina Rossetti: A Biographical and Critical Study.* 4th ed. London, 1898.

Birkhead, Edith. *Christina Rossetti and Her Poetry.* London, 1930.

Bowra, C. M. "Christina Rossetti." In *The Romantic Imagination.* Cambridge, Mass., 1949.

Brzenk, Eugene J. "'Up-Hill' and 'Down-' by Christina Rossetti." *Victorian Poetry,* X (1972), 367–71.

Burdett, Osbert. *The Beardsley Period: An Essay in Perspective.* New York, 1925.

Crump, R. W., ed. *The Complete Poems of Christina Rossetti: A Variorum Edition.* 2 vols. to date. Baton Rouge, 1979, 1986.

Curran, Stuart. "The Lyric Voice of Christina Rossetti." *Victorian Poetry,* IX (1971), 287–99.

DeVitis, A. A. "'Goblin Market': Fairy Tale and Reality." *Journal of Popular Culture,* I (1968), 418–26.

Doughty, Oswald. *A Victorian Romantic: Dante Gabriel Rossetti.* London, 1949.

Doughty, Oswald, and John Robert Wahl, eds. *Letters of Dante Gabriel Rossetti.* 4 vols. Oxford, 1967.

Evans, B. Ifor. *English Poetry in the Later Nineteenth Century.* 2nd ed. New York, 1966.

————. "The Sources of Christina Rossetti's 'Goblin Market.'" *Modern Language Review,* XXVIII (1933), 156–65.

Ford, Ford Madox. *Memories and Impressions: A Study in Atmospheres.* New York, 1911.

Fredeman, William E. "*Christina Rossetti,* by Lona Mosk Packer." *Victorian Studies,* VIII (1964), 71–77.

————. "The Pre-Raphaelites." In *The Victorian Poets: A Guide to Research,* edited by Frederic E. Faverty. 2nd ed. Cambridge, Mass., 1968.

Gilbert, Sandra M., and Susan Gubar. *The Madwoman in the Attic: The Woman Writer and the Nineteenth Century Literary Imagination.* New Haven, 1979.

Going, William T. "'Goblin Market' and the Pre-Raphaelite Brotherhood." *Pre-Raphaelite Review,* III (1979), 54–62.

Golub, Ellen. "Untying Goblin Apron Strings: A Psychoanalytic Reading of 'Goblin Market.'" *Literature and Psychology,* XXV (1975), 158–65.

Greer, Germaine. Introduction to *Goblin Market,* by Christina Rossetti. New York, 1975.

Greg, William Rathbone. *Literary and Social Judgments.* Boston, 1873.

Harrison, Antony H. "Christina Rossetti: The Poetic Vocation." *Texas Studies in Literature and Language,* XXVII (1985), 225–46.

————. *Christina Rossetti in Context.* Chapel Hill, 1988.

Hickok, Kathleen. *Representations of Women: Nineteenth-Century British Women's Poetry.* Westport, Conn., 1984.

Hill, Robert W., Jr., ed. *Tennyson's Poetry.* New York, 1971.

Hönnighausen, Gisela. "Emblematic Tendencies in the Works of Christina Rossetti." *Victorian Poetry,* X (1972), 1–15.

Houghton, Walter E., and G. Robert Stange, eds. *Victorian Poetry and Poetics.* Boston, 1959. 2nd ed., 1968.

Hueffer, Ford Madox. "The Collected Poems of Christina Rossetti." *Fortnightly Review,* o.s. LXXXI (1904), 393–405.

Jennings, Elizabeth, ed. *A Choice of Christina Rossetti's Verse.* London, 1970.

Keble, John. *Lectures on Poetry.* Translated by E. K. Francis. 2 vols. Oxford, 1912.

————. *Tracts for the Times.* London, 1833–1841.

Kent, Muriel. "Christina Rossetti: A Reconsideration." *Contemporary Review,* CXXXVIII (1930), 759–67.

Kohl, James A. "A Medical Comment on Christina Rossetti." *Notes and Queries,* CCXIII (1968), 423–24.

Lang, Cecil. *The Pre-Raphaelites and Their Circle.* Boston, 1968.

Lasner, Mark Samuels. "Christina Rossetti's 'Common Looking Booklet': A Newsletter about her *Verses* of 1847." *Notes and Queries,* CCXXVI (1981), 420–21.

Macmillan, George A., ed. *Letters of Alexander Macmillan.* Glasgow, 1908.

McGann, Jerome J. "Christina Rossetti's Poems: A New Edition and a Revaluation." *Victorian Studies,* XXIII (1980), 237–54.

————. "The Religious Poetry of Christina Rossetti." *Critical Inquiry,* X (1983), 127–44.

Mermin, Dorothy. "Heroic Sisterhood in 'Goblin Market.' " *Victorian Poetry,* XXI (1983), 107–18.

Michie, Helena. "The Battle for Sisterhood: Christina Rossetti's Strategies for Control in Her Sister Poems." *Journal of Pre-Raphaelite Studies,* III (1983), 38–55.

Moers, Ellen. *Literary Women: The Great Writers.* Garden City, N.Y., 1976.

More, Paul E., ed. *The Complete Poetical Works of Byron.* Boston, 1905.

Newman, John Henry. *Apologia pro vita sua.* Edited by Martin Svaglic. Oxford, 1967.

Noble, James Ashcroft. *Impressions and Memories.* London, 1895.

Packer, Lona Mosk. *Christina Rossetti.* Berkeley, 1963.

————. "Symbol and Reality in Christina Rossetti's *Goblin Market.*" *Publications of the Modern Language Association,* LXXIII (1958), 375–85.

————, ed. *The Rossetti-Macmillan Letters.* Berkeley, 1963.

Preston, Harriet Waters, ed. *The Complete Poetical Works of Elizabeth Barrett Browning.* Boston, 1900.

Rees, Joan. "Christina Rossetti: Poet." *Critical Quarterly,* XXVI (1984), 59–72.

Rosenblum, Dolores. "Christina Rossetti: The Inward Pose." In *Shakespeare's Sisters: Feminist Essays on Women Poets,* edited by Sandra M. Gilbert and Susan Gubar. Bloomington, Ind., 1979.

————. *Christina Rossetti: The Poetry of Endurance.* Carbondale, Ill., 1986.

————. "Christina Rossetti's Poetry: Watching, Looking, Keeping Vigil." *Victorian Poetry,* XX (1982), 33–49.

Rossetti, Christina. *Maude: Prose and Verse.* Chicago, 1897.

————. *Time Flies: A Reading Diary.* London, 1890.

————. *Verses.* London, 1893.

Rossetti, William Michael. *Some Reminiscences of William Michael Rossetti*. 2 vols. New York, 1906.

————, ed. *The Family Letters of Christina Georgina Rossetti*. London, 1908.

————, ed. *The Poetical Works of Christina Georgina Rossetti*. London, 1904.

Sagan, Miriam. "Christina Rossetti's 'Goblin Market' and Feminist Literary Criticism." *Pre-Raphaelite Review,* III (1980), 66–76.

Sandars, Mary F. *The Life of Christina Rossetti*. London, 1930.

Schiller, Friedrich. *The Poems of Schiller*. Translated by E. P. Arnold-Forster. London, 1903.

Stevenson, Lionel. *The Pre-Raphaelite Poets*. Chapel Hill, 1972.

Swann, Thomas Burnett. *Wonder and Whimsey: The Fantastic World of Christina Rossetti*. Francestown, N.H., 1960.

Tennyson, G. B. *Victorian Devotional Poetry: The Tractarian Mode*. Cambridge, Mass., 1980.

Thomas, Eleanor Walter. *Christina Georgina Rossetti*. New York, 1931.

von der Hellen, Eduard, ed. *Schillers Samtliche Werke*. Vol. I of 8 vols. Stuttgart, 1904.

Waller, John O. "Christ's Second Coming: Christina Rossetti and the Premillennialist William Dodsworth." *Bulletin of the New York Public Library,* LXXIII (1969), 465–82.

Waller, R. D. *The Rossetti Family: 1823–1854*. Manchester, 1932.

Weintraub, Stanley. *Four Rossettis: A Victorian Biography*. New York, 1977.

Woolf, Virginia. *The Common Reader: Second Series*. London, 1932.

Index